DAYBREAKERS

Friendships
with
Muslim Women

LaVonda Malone

MIO Frontiers
Phoenix, Arizona 85026

Daybreakers / Friendships with Muslim Women
Copyright ©2006 by MIO Frontiers

Published by MIO Frontiers
P.O. Box 60670
Phoenix, AZ 85026-0670
www.Frontiers.org

ISBN 0-9788907-0-1

Cover Design by Mark Sequeira
MJA Studios, 2006

Printed in the United States of America

Contents

Acknowledgments

I have found that it takes a good number of people working together to produce a book. Therefore, I owe thanks to many. First, my sincere thanks to Bob Blincoe, U.S. Director of Frontiers, for commissioning me to do the book.

For years, working at the office, I heard fascinating stories from the field, especially about Muslim women. Their lives are particularly hard and filled with suffering. It's exciting to see the impact our field women are making in the lives of these women, and I wanted to share their stories with others. Bob Blincoe gave me that exciting opportunity.

I owe many thanks to the missionary women who took time to share their personal stories, stories that will give you a rare, intimate look into the lives, cultures and customs of Muslim women in many parts of the world. Due to the nature of our work, we cannot disclose the real names or specific locations of the missionary nor the names of the Muslims involved in these stories. We do make an exception for retired field missionary, Edna Lewis, whom we wish to honor.

My heartfelt appreciation goes to Julia Colgate, experienced field missionary, whose encouragement early on in the project was so meaningful to me. I also owe countless thanks to Sheila Brunty for proof-reading and assisting in editing the manuscript. My sincere thanks goes to Sheryl Johnston for a final review of the work. Many accolades go to Mark Sequeira for the cover design and his professionalism in making the book better. Finally, I give special mention to my dear sister, Norma Crosby, for her wonderful enthusiasm and joy in the project.

We trust that *Daybreakers* will inform, edify and inspire you to pray for those who do not know they sit in great darkness.

Preface

First of all, *Daybreakers* is a credit to the many wonderful women who have contributed to the book and whose personal experiences it portrays. Their stories are a tribute to their perseverance, sacrifice, and deep love for the lost. Compiled into this one small book are many years of combined field experience. Each story gives an intimate look into the culture of Islam, showing life by life, experience by experience, the great impact that Christian friendship has made in the lives of Muslim women.

Not all of these can be called "success" stories. But that is the way real life is, both here at home and on the field. Just by being there, by being "salt and light," our workers make a difference.

Muslims are among the most devoutly religious people on earth; yet despite prayers five times a day and strict adherence to religious doctrine, they do not understand the way of salvation. They do not know the joy of walking with our Lord, nor do they have any assurance of heaven when they die.

We believe that a great day is dawning on the Muslim world and that we are blessed by God to be of great use to Him in His redemptive work.

I have made you a light for the nations,

That you may bring salvation to the ends of the earth.

(Acts 13:47 English Standard Version, paraphrased)

La Vonda Malone

Abandoned Babies

Story by Patricia

Patricia, her husband, and their ten-year-old son have been on the field in North Africa for several years. Her all-consuming passion and joy is caring for unwanted, cast-off babies, deemed unadoptable, having been born out of wedlock and considered "sin." The babies receive absolutely minimal care from the hospital staff. Patricia and several of her friends have become the infants' devoted surrogate mothers. Here is her heart-breaking story of the "abandoned babies."

How can I ever describe the emotion of sympathy and pity I felt for those wailing infants the first time I walked into the hospital with friends to help care for the "abandoned babies?" I wanted to swoop up them all into my arms at once and comfort them, to hold them and sing to them. There they were, dozens of babies, with their cribs lined up out in the hallway. All were from one day to three months old, each one crying out for its needs to be met–to be fed, to be diapered, to be turned over, or just to be touched–and no one was doing it!

You may ask, "Abandoned babies! Who would do that? Whose

babies are these? How did they come to be here? Why are they abandoned? Why aren't they being better cared for?" The majority of these infants are born to unwed mothers who come to the hospital to give birth. In the culture of the country I live in, unwed mothers are not allowed, by family or society, to keep their newborns. The children are considered to be "sin" and therefore outcasts, worthy of only minimal care. Some of the babies are born elsewhere and brought to the hospital by relatives. Others are brought there because their families are just too poor to care for them. These actually are the luckier ones, because they at least are deemed to be adoptable, while the ones born to unwed mothers are not. When the babies are about three months old they are taken to an orphanage where they remain until they reach adulthood.

At the hospital there are two departments for infants. One is the regular nursery where legitimate babies are well cared for. The other is out in the hall where the "abandoned babies" are kept. The number of these infants can range from five to 35. Although the babies are not well cared for by the nursing staff, the nurses feel no guilt or responsibility. They feed the babies every four hours by propping up a bottle in their mouths but give no physical touch. When they do touch them, it's only to do a routine diaper change several times a day. Often we will find a three- or four-month-old very lethargic because the baby has never been out of its crib except when we are there to hold it. The babies have never seen colors. At times we have brought in mobiles for their cribs or something to stimulate them, but the items are stolen immediately, usually by the staff. We've learned to bring things with us and take them home again until our next visit. One of my goals for the coming year is to have a stereo to take with me so the babies can hear music when we come.

It's necessary to have a lot of grace with the nurses because it is so engrained in them that these babies have no worth. It has touched them to see us coming in and treating the babies like the little treasures they are. In fact, we have observed some improvements. At times , a nurse will come in and talk to us and stand next to a crib and actually touch one of the babies! Or they will hold the bottle rather than just prop it up. We have even seen one nurse, a young girl, pick up a baby! And she seems to have much compassion and love. We are praying that little by little the hearts of the nursing staff will be changed. That is where there will be a long-term change. If the nursing staff can be filled with God's love and compassion, they will share that with the babies. "May God make it so" is our prayer.

Wasella's Miracle

Story #2 by Patricia

One day I was quite alone in caring for the "abandoned" babies, when a young woman came in and asked if she could pick up her child. I said "Yes," not knowing this was frowned upon or perhaps not even allowed. She went right over to a crib and picked up a little baby boy. She was obviously so in love with this baby; it was apparent that he was a part of her.

Although it was a very cold day outside and she came in very warmly dressed, she was so involved with the baby that she never bothered to take off any outer clothing, no matter how uncomfortable it became for her. She sat there for two hours just crying over the baby and loving him. Then she asked if she could feed him. When the baby finished feeding she went back to crying and weeping over the child and saying over and over in her dialect, "Oh, what am I going to do? What am I going to do?"

It was obvious that she loved this baby so much and was in much agony being apart from him. I sat down next to her, hoping in some way to comfort her. I listened to her as she told her story. She said she was not married and her family forbade her to keep the baby because she had sinned. After listening to her for awhile, I asked her what

4

her name was and if I could pray for her. She told me her name was Wasella but that she did not understand what I meant when I said I would like to pray for her. In her culture, that is not a normal thing to do. I said to her, "Right now, Wasella, I would like to pray for you and your baby." And she agreed to let me pray for her. I prayed the only way I knew how in that situation and asked God for a miracle! I could see the love she had for her baby and I knew this child deserved his mother and her love. So I prayed for Wasella and her son. I did not know what the outcome of that prayer would be, but I earnestly prayed for a miracle!

I went home that day and sent about 150 e-mails to praying friends, asking them to pray for a miracle. Right away I started getting responses as to how this story had touched people's hearts and how they had started praying for a miracle for Wasella.

The next time I went to the hospital, one of the nursing staff, who usually won't even talk to us, said, "This little boy is leaving us."

I said, "Oh! Is he going to the orphanage?"

"No, he is going home", she replied. "His mother and father have been coming every day to see the baby, and they are getting married. The family is blessing it all and they are taking the baby home!"

Wasella got her miracle! Within two weeks of the time I first met her, she was married to the man she loved and was a full-time mom to her beloved baby. Since the day I met her and prayed for her, I have had no contact with her. I don't know where she lives or anything more about her except that she is with her husband and baby and that she has her family's blessing. What joy that brings to my heart!

One thing I am certain of–Wasella knows that it was God who performed this lovely miracle for her. I pray this is just the beginning of her trusting Him more.

Esther's Journey Begins

Story by Esther

Esther is a single young European woman whose chosen country of service is in the Middle East. In this interview she shares with us how she recently came to be on this journey to another land so different in culture from her own. She tells why she gave up family, a good career, and all that was familiar to her to spend and be spent, and to bear burdens that are not her own for the sake of Christ.

Interviewer: Tell me, Esther, how did you become interested in your chosen country?

Esther: My professional job in my own country was as a social worker. I had worked at that job for over five years. During that time I served many people from the Middle East, including many from the country I am now called to. I grew to know them and to love them. When I first felt God's call to this particular country, I tried to reason with Him and said to Him, "Well, Lord, I am already serving this people. Why do I need to go to their country? Can't I just continue to serve them here?" And the Lord said, "No. You must go there in person. My grace is sufficient." He continued to deal with me and even gave me the name of a city where I was to serve. At last I yielded to His call and made my plans to go.

Interviewer: What were your first steps in preparation to go?

Esther: I first decided to go there and "check it out." So I went there on a four month visa, and I really felt that was where God wanted me to be.

Interviewer: Were you connected with some of the Frontiers team serving in that country before you went on that exploratory trip?

Esther: Yes. Through e-mail I got acquainted with some of the team with whom I would be working. I met the rest of the team later at our International Conference in England.

Interviewer: Tell us something of interest about that first trip.

Esther: My language helper, Hakima, and I became good friends. I was teaching her English and she was teaching me her language. She was very open and gracious to me. I learned about some of the bondage she was in, and I was deeply touched. When she was pregnant with one of her children, her brother died in a foreign country in a drowning accident. The family decided to keep it from her because of her pregnancy. When she found out about it sometime later, she cursed the baby she was carrying because her pregnancy prevented her from going to the funeral. To this day she does not love that child. This, of course, causes her guilt and pain, and she is an unhappy person. I hope to minister to her further when I return to that country.

Interviewer: What about the dress code in your country?

Esther: Women everywhere are usually concerned about choosing what to wear. In this country, choosing is not an option. Whenever we go on the street, we wear an overcoat (regardless of the weather) called a mantle. A head scarf is always worn. I don't really mind–it is something one gets used to. Underneath the coat, jeans or a skirt can be worn, but it is always necessary to wear that covering.

Interviewer: What do young women there do for fun?

Esther: They really like to dance! The dance is that shimmy-and-shake kind of dance. Of course, it's always girls with girls. Even at weddings men and women don't dance together, unless it is the bride and groom or perhaps some older married couple. We women sometimes go in a group shopping or to a restaurant. I have found it rather easy to make friends with people there. They are very gracious to invite us into their homes.

Interviewer: What about religion? Do they like to discuss it?

Esther: We do talk about religion, but it is very hard for them to see God as Father. They see that as blasphemous. They believe that Allah does not have a personal relationship with people. Islam teaches that God does not reveal Himself to anyone in any way, that God only reveals His will in the Qur'an.

Interviewer: Now that you have decided to go there long term, what is your next step?

Esther: I have enrolled in an internship program here in the U.S. for six months prior to my going to the field to join the team.

Interviewer: Was it difficult for your family to give you up?

Esther: Yes and no. It was more difficult for my mother. She said, "Why disturb those people? Why do you need to go? They have their own religion and they are quite happy with it." Her reply surprised me a bit, but it did certainly reflect the attitude of a great many people when it comes to missions. I pray for her deeper spiritual understanding. My dad's attitude was quite different. He said, "This is between you and God. If you must go, then go, with my blessings." I was blessed by his attitude.

Interviewer: Is it hard to leave family and friends?

Esther: No. After spending more time with the entire team recently, I already feel an important kinship with my teammates.

Interviewer: Now that you have come this far toward your goal, learning to love the people you will be serving, visiting their homeland, and making preparations to go to the field, what are your final thoughts?

Esther: Sometimes I am uncertain of the next step, but I am certain of God. He packs my life with surprises all the time. It is with great joy and anticipation that I begin this journey and go out into the future with Him!

Mira: Atheist

Story by Lisa

Lisa is a young woman who has been serving Muslims in Eastern Europe for the past eight years. She has organized a successful women's prison ministry. However, what Lisa chose to share with us in this publication is her everyday life with her neighbors.

In my adopted country I live in a major city, a city made up of apartment dwellers. The city builds up, not out, so virtually everyone lives in an apartment building. There is almost a class distinction between those who live in an apartment building with an elevator or one without. For years I had lived in apartments without elevators. Then circumstances changed so that I chose an apartment building with an elevator. At first I was worried about making friends with people, as I had heard many stories about how difficult it was to get to know your neighbors in that environment. But God opened the doors and I have been able to get to know my neighbors, especially Mira and Beni.

Although they were born into Muslim families, they had become hard-core atheists, not worshiping God at all. They had fully embraced Communism, having been under that regime for many years. Because of what they had been through, they actually saw the Communist party as a liberator. Both were involved in party leadership and knew many people of the higher echelon.

God kept nudging me to go visit them, and so I went. I can't say I was not apprehensive about it. But they were very gracious and receptive to me. Mira told me later that I was the only person her husband had ever allowed to speak about God in their home. Mira had problems with her heart, and often when I went to visit, she would be lying on the sofa, ill, sometimes with a fever. God would have me pray for her and she would get better. This happened several times. One day Beni came over to my apartment on the pretense of borrowing an orange to get me to pray for Mira. So I went and prayed for her, and I sang to her just to let her know that Jesus loves her. And she got better. They were now at the point where they expected she would get better when I came and prayed, while I, on the other hand, was always surprised but just obeying God.

Another time Beni came to get me to pray for Mira, but I couldn't come as I had company. I told him that even though I couldn't come at that time that I would still pray. So from that moment I started praying for her. Later, when I did get there, she said she had started feeling better at that time. This was my opportunity to impress upon her that it was God and not me who was healing her. I said, "See, it is Jesus who does it. It is Jesus who came before me and healed you." And I think she really began to understand that it was Jesus who was healing her. I gave her a few books to read and we had some conversations about God.

One day Mira fell and broke her hip. Because she was in her seventies, this was very serious. She came home from the hospital but was not doing well. She had lost all hope of recovery and was refusing to eat. It was a form of slow suicide by starvation. She looked so very bad that I realized this might well be my last opportunity to speak to her about salvation. It was made more difficult by the fact that in this culture, one does not talk about death to the dying. That is considered very impolite! Also, the nurse was in the room, and she indicated I should not be talking to Mira about God. However, Mira's son, standing nearby, gave me the go-ahead. So I continued to pray with great enthusiasm for her, trusting God to guide my words, forgetting about the family. After my prayer the nurse again took her pulse and said it was much better and even sat Mira up a bit! So I left her that day.

When I came back a few days later, Mira was much better. And she had started eating! I knew this was an act of her will, and it showed me she had hope. In fact, she said to me, "Lisa, I now have hope." Her character had also changed. Being a great complainer before, she stopped complaining so much. One day I was talking with her nurse about having a relationship with God when Mira chimed in and was avidly agreeing that God is close and intimate with us. I could see that she was growing in her understanding of God's love and that it was not just head knowledge but heart knowledge. Her heart had come to life!

What is so exciting to me is that God doesn't give up on us. He keeps on pursuing us and communicating with us. He knew of Mira's need that came from her atheistic background. She needed to see God act supernaturally. Our all-wise God started at the very center of her need, her physical healing, and worked from there to reach her intellect and her spirit. God met her needs in every way!

I left on furlough for America soon after this, but I am praying that when I return to my adopted country, I will find Mira thriving and happy in the Lord. And I pray that her life and experience with the Lord will now speak Life into her whole family, and Jesus will bring Light to them also.

Fatima: My Unlikely Friend
Story by Louisa

Louisa and her husband have worked among Muslims in Africa for ten years. They have two daughters. She tells a story of an unlikely friendship with a Palestinian woman. Louisa says that what they had in common was more significant than their differences.

Fatima and I were unlikely friends from the outset. She is not a member of the majority ethnic group here in our country, nor is she of the minority ethnic group among whom we minister. In fact, she is far from home, living here in our town as an exile. Fatima is Palestinian. Because Americans and Palestinians are usually divided by an immense wall of misunderstanding built on politics, it was surprising to find Fatima becoming my friend. Yet, by opening the door to me in unexpected friendship, she brought me to a new understanding of her people's culture and history.

Fatima and her husband were heavily involved in politics, in "the struggle against the oppressors" as they call it, to the point of spending time in Israeli jails. Fatima's husband is now prohibited from returning to Palestine. Fatima and their two children joined him in exile in order to keep their family together. Fatima and her husband are always warmly hospitable in welcoming me to their home. They insist that the hospitality they show me here is little compared to what they would show me in their home country. I have an open invitation to visit them in Palestine as soon as they are allowed to return. Obviously, it's a bit of a contradiction that this family is so generous to someone who as a westerner might be considered hostile to their people. But what we share is more significant than what divides us. Perhaps one of the things that drew us together was that both of us are living far from our native countries and feel the loss of connections to our extended families.

As our friendship grew, I learned some of the story of her life. I was struck by the difficult road she has walked. I once asked Fatima if she had any idea, when she fell in love and married her husband, of the kind of life that awaited them. The repeated separations, imprisonments, danger and uncertainty must have stressed their relationship. She had a quick answer: "We met each other at a student demonstration. We knew from the beginning that we were completely dedicated to the Palestinian cause. That has kept us together."

I asked her if she worried about the safety of her relatives living in the Palestinian Territories, where the violence of conflict claims so many lives. "Oh, no," she said. "We are all ready to be martyrs. We Palestinians are raised to be martyrs for our people and our land. It's an honor."

But then one day Fatima got the news that a nephew of hers had been killed. It was several weeks before I saw her without red, swollen eyes; it was clear that her grief was real and deep. This was just one of the many ways in which contradictions were woven into the fabric of Fatima's life.

As our friendship deepened, she was ready to open up to me about the reality of stress. She told me, "Actually, I have often felt anxious. When I do, I go shopping. I buy myself gold jewelry." Here were more seemingly contradictory threads woven into this unique woman's life.

Despite holding firmly to different faiths, Fatima and I have been able to talk about God and His meaning in our lives. She is a devout Muslim, but she knows I am praying for her. The last time we visited, she expressed hope that they will soon be able to return home, as a result of the ongoing peace process. I remember how her eyes shone when she talked about her home, its beauty, its traditions, and its history.

She says that when I visit Palestine, she will take me to the places where Jesus lived, taught, and performed miracles. She told me, "Everywhere you go in Palestine, you smell Jesus. The smell of Him is all around." I think of this every time I pray for Fatima. No matter where her turbulent life takes her, may she smell Jesus all around. May she be unable to ignore Him until she turns to Him for the peace she has been seeking all her life.

Tea Time

An Invitation To Tea

Story by Andrea

Andrea and her husband have lived in Asia for seven years. They have four children. In the first of her two interesting stories, Andrea has been invited to her national friend's home for tea. She allows you the privilege of entering her host's home and sharing tea-time with her hospitable friends.

I met Miriam when she was a student of my husband's at the university where he was teaching. She and her mother came to visit me and bring a gift after the birth of one of my children. Immediately upon meeting me, they embraced me and loved me, which is very unusual here. In Asia marriages and births are special events and give women an opportunity to visit each other. Once they had visited me, then their home was open to me to return the visit.

We are well acquainted now and I have made many visits to their house for tea. Today, as usual, there are several women in the house, Miriam, her sister and her mother. Sometimes other women of the family or from the neighborhood will join us. After they warmly greet me, we seat ourselves on the floor which is covered by an ornate rug. Large comfortable pillows surround us.

One woman of the household will usually do the serving. Today Miriam's mother is doing the honor. She starts bringing out food on a large decorative tray. Juice is always served first. They, being a family of modest means, serve juice from a carton. If they were a really wealthy family, it probably would be fresh-squeezed orange juice or pomegranate juice. Next, she brings out little cakes and cookies. Occasionally something savory will be served, but not today. Now the server brings out a big bowl of fruit. She cuts it up and puts some on a plate in front of me. They just keep serving it until at some point you have to decline. I have learned, over the years, those families who will and will not be offended if I refuse food. Thankfully, this family is not one who will be offended if I decline to eat everything offered me.

Coffee, a favorite, is served in tiny cups. When I have had enough, I don't say, "No, thank you." Instead, I just wiggle my little finger with the cup turned upside down, and that gives them a visual signal that I've had enough. (Also this allows the conversation to continue uninterrupted.) Tea is usually served in small, slender glasses rather than in a cup. The most popular is "milk tea". It is just regular black tea with canned milk, served with a lot of sugar and sometimes with mint.

Talk usually revolves around our immediate families. Sometimes we will talk about religion. I have often shared with them my experiences of answered prayer. However, they are not open to the Gospel in a personal way. They are very quick to say that Islam and Christianity are so similar, saying something like, "You're okay.

You're a Christian and I love you. And we're Muslim and we're okay. We all believe in God."

Several pleasant hours have now passed and it is time to go. I invite them to come to my house for tea, but more often than not I will go to their house where they are more comfortable. We say our sweet good-byes until our next visit.

They are a lovely, hospitable family, but the time came when I asked God if I should invest more time in this family because of their lack of openness to the Gospel. It wasn't long before God gave me a spiritual dream, at the end of which I saw Miriam's brother. He smiled at me and said, "Merry Christmas." And then the dream ended. I sensed in my spirit that his saying that was significant, because, of course, Muslims do not celebrate Christmas. I felt that this was my signal not to give up on this family.

Still, I wanted further conformation. So I asked God to allow me, on my next visit to their home, to at least see and speak to the brother, something which seldom happened on my visits. When I went to their home, the person who opened the door and greeted me was the brother! We exchanged greetings–that was all. But then, that was all I had asked for. So I continue to visit with and pray for this family. I know that God is leading me, and my job is to follow that lead and to trust Him for the outcome.

"For we walk by faith, not by sight." (II Cor. 5:7 KJV)

"Sarah Laughing"

Story #2 by Andrea

In the Arab nation where I gladly serve, a woman has two ways to achieve honor and status in the society. First, she can be married, which elevates her in a way that a single woman cannot achieve. Second, as a married woman, she can give birth–becoming a mother further increases her status.

Among the Muslim friends I cherish is a woman I'll call "Sarah." Married for many years, Sarah had been unable to conceive. This caused her constant emotional grief; it was clear that she suffered in many ways by being childless.

When I was leaving for a home ministry assignment in the U.S., I asked many of my Muslim friends, including Sarah, how I could pray for them while I was away for several months. When I asked Sarah how I could pray for her, this was her answer: "I will not tell you how to pray for me because friends know how to pray for friends. I don't need to tell you."

I knew she was right. As her close friend, I already knew her deepest desire and greatest wish was that she might become pregnant, bear a child, and be a mother.

Since Sarah had not told me her prayer request, I also did not tell her how I would be praying. But of course, during my time in the U.S., I prayed for Sarah, that she might conceive and bear a child. While I was visiting my home church and touring other churches as well, I asked several of my close friends to pray for Sarah–to ask God to touch her and allow her to bear children.

After I returned to my home in the Arab nation where I serve, among the first people I saw was Sarah–and she was joyously, radiantly pregnant! Sarah was glowing.

It was only then that I confessed to her: "Sarah, my prayer for you was that God would bless you with a child!"

Sarah laughed with joy.

She soon gave birth to a little boy, and has since borne two more children. Now a contented and happy mother of three, Sarah often laughs with me about all this. And it is she who reminds me that all of this happened because God answered prayer. Sarah knows that God opened her womb. She knows who has blessed her.

Now will you join me in praying that Sarah experiences a 'new birth' and accepts Jesus as her Messiah and Lord?

"Why? Why? Why?"

Story by Marcie

A year ago Marcie went with one of our teams to serve six months in a Middle Eastern country. The team lived together in a rented house in a residential neighborhood. Just two weeks after Marcie arrived, her next door neighbor, Mr. Barak, died suddenly of a heart attack. Marcie tells how she and her teammates, through this tragic event, came to love and be loved by this family.

This morning, the father of the dear family that lives next door died of a heart attack. Around 11:00 a.m. we noticed a lot of people outside and many cars on the street and in front of our house. My teammate, Jennifer, went outside to ask a neighbor what was happening. He told her the father had died.

We both responded with an unbelieving, "What, the father next door?" It was true. This man who invited us into the warmth of his home our first night here, when we had just moved in and had no electricity, water, or heaters; this man who tracked down the electrician late one cold night to fix our electricity; who came to our rescue when we needed translation with men working on our house; whose two dear sons have become like brothers to us; whose wife invited us to spend the night at their house when we were cold and had no heaters; who lent us ladders, drills, and hammers and who helped us work on our house; who insisted that we ask him for help when we needed anything–this man who had taken care of us for our first two weeks here was now suddenly gone!

I stayed at home to watch my team-mate's children while she went next door to see the grieving family. When she returned, I headed next door alone. Lots of men stood outside the house and in the street. I walked nervously through them to get to the front door. Standing near the door was Salmad, the 25-year-old son who had become my sweet brother. Tears wet his face and he looked at me with hopeless eyes. My heart crashed to the floor to see him in such pain.

"Do you want to go in?" he asked me quietly. He led me to the living room where all the women were gathered. The room was filled with the sounds of weeping and the covered heads of the Muslim women. On the couch to my left, I saw Sara, the oldest daughter. I sat next to her. "Oh Marcie!" she exclaimed as she embraced me. In her deep sorrow she repeated the word for her father, "Oh, my Baba. My Baba!" I put my arm tightly around her back, and she put her head on my shoulder. We cried together. Then she very clearly spoke an English word that will always haunt me, "Why? Why? Why?"

For the next two hours I sat on that couch next to her. She got the Qur'an off the shelf and fumbled to find the page she wanted. She held it to her face and kissed it. As she read she began to weep again. I wondered what it said. I prayed our Scriptures over her and her family. I prayed and prayed and prayed. Many more women came and filled the room with loud wailing. Their mourning was very expressive. I couldn't help but cry as I saw their hopeless sadness. The mother sat on the floor, melting under the intensity of her sorrow. Many verses came to my mind:

Rejoice with those who rejoice; mourn with those who mourn. (Romans 12:15)

The Lord is close to the brokenhearted and saves those who are crushed in spirit. (Psalm 34:18)

He heals the brokenhearted and binds up their wounds. (Psalm 143:7)

Never again will they hunger; never again will they thirst. The sun will not beat upon them, nor any scorching heat. For the Lamb at the center of the throne will be their shepherd, he will lead them to springs of living water. And God will wipe every tear from their eyes. (Revelation 7:16-17)

He will swallow up death forever. The Sovereign Lord will wipe away the tears from all faces; he will remove the disgrace of his people from all the earth. (Isaiah 25:8)

My team members and I mourn for this man because he did not die with hope of eternal life with Christ. It is difficult to fathom the ramifications of that. All I can think is that the length of our remaining time with these people is unknown. I must do the work while there is life. They must hear and know.

Oh, Jesus, have mercy upon this place. Help me to tell the story to the perishing while they still have life.

Days Of Mourning

Story #2 by Marcie

Mr. Barak died on December 29th. For the next five days the entire extended family on both sides gathered at the house. It was turned into a perpetual gathering place for family, friends and neighbors- women in one room and men in another. People were there night and day, as it is considered very bad for the widow to be alone at this time. Mourning is done in community. There is no sense of needing privacy or solitude during this time in this culture. We joined them that first day, and with much love they requested that we return for the following three days of traditional mourning. What occurred over those next few days was so precious to me that I only hope I can communicate the awe of it all.

In the days that followed we were introduced to all six children and their spouses and children, and to every uncle and aunt and cousin and their spouses and children and then lots of extra relatives that I couldn't keep straight. Anyone who had any connection whatsoever to any family member, through blood or marriage, was considered "family." For those five days I spent about six hours each day at the house just sitting in the "women's room," eating meals and talking with the sisters and cousins, and just falling in love with this family. Our hearts were knit together in those days.

But what I really want to share is that God used the death of the father to enable us to meet the entire family and to be welcomed into the most intimate part of their family life. From death truly came life, the life of our deep friendship. Without this tragic event, we would not have had an opportunity to meet the whole extended family. Our connection with this family would never have reached such rich depths without weeping with them and loving them through this tragedy.

When we'd leave each afternoon, they'd ask us to return in the evening after all the neighbors and friends had gone. That was so significant to us because that was a specifically designated time just for the family to be together. We would sit in the living room with all the family, men and women together, since it was just family, and talk and laugh and look at their old family pictures. Most of them spoke some English, but a lot of our communication was non-verbal and simply between our hearts.

On the evening before the third day, when they prepare a big lunch for everyone, we were sitting with the family as usual and the women began to bring many bags of vegetables out onto a mat on the floor to prepare them for the dolma they would make for the next day. Dolma is a special ethnic dish that takes a lot of time to prepare and tastes delicious. A great chasm of relationship was bridged when the women motioned for Rebecca, my roommate, and me to kneel on the floor next to them and help them prepare the food. With huge smiles on our faces we knelt next to them and peeled and cut vegetables while we all laughed and reveled in the moment. We were no longer guests of honor sitting off at a distance, but sisters in their family, kneeling on the floor and getting dirt under our finger nails just as they were. We departed in the evening with many kisses and sweet expressions of love. Each day our bond grew as we walked with them on the path of sorrow.

The next afternoon as I was helping the mother serve lunch, she stopped and started crying. I wrapped my arms around her and said nothing as she wept. It was just one of those moments when the sorrow just hit her. I only pray that she feels Jesus in my embrace and senses His peace through me. It is times like this when I know I didn't just happen to be in the kitchen–but that my steps were directed to be available to be Jesus to her in her moment of heartbreak. My team also didn't just happen to move next door to this particular family only two weeks before their father died. We were destined before the world began to be here at this time. Our Father has perfect timing!

Member Of The Family

Story #3 by Marcie

Here Marcie recounts a memorable evening with her next door neighbors, the Barak family. She becomes an insider, an accepted member of the family.

I came home from the neighbors with a full heart and a satisfied smile. Rebecca, my roommate, and I had gone over for a visit around 7:00 p.m. I had intended to stay only briefly, as I hadn't been feeling well that week. Rebecca went home after about 30 minutes, but since I then felt okay, I stayed–and stayed. They eat dinner very late, usually around 10:00 p.m., so they insisted I stay to eat. And I am so happy that I did, because we did something we had never done before–a barbecue in the backyard! It was such fun and turned out to be a time I will treasure forever. We pulled the table and chairs from the kitchen to the outside, and one brother made kabobs on a little grill. They turned on music, and the kids giggled as they gathered bunches of flowers. We all relaxed under the stars while a cool summer breeze refreshed us after a long week.

Lately, I have felt that everyone in the family is grouchy or mad about something, and it hasn't been very pleasant to spend time at their house. Because of their bad attitudes, I've really had to push myself to go spend time with them. Our relationship has progressed to that stage where no one wears masks anymore. There have been family fights and spats between spouses right in front of me. They don't hide from me what is really going on within the family. One would suppose it would be a blessing to be more on the inside of the family, but it has been burdensome to me to see the conflict and gossip and attitudes.

But this night was different. Maybe it was the change of scenery or the cool breeze or the yummy food, but everyone was in a good mood! We talked and laughed and just enjoyed being together.

Everyone knew I was going home in a week. So, the inevitable question on everyone's lips was, "Are you coming back?" The best answer I could give them was, "I don't know. Inshallah" (Arabic for "if God wills"). They've asked this question for months now, and I always give them this same answer. They keep asking it though, maybe hoping my answer will turn to a "yes." "Don't go. We will miss you," they said with sad voices, putting a gentle hand on my arm and looking me in the eyes. I always have to look away when they do that. It's just too much for me.

After we ate, I helped clear the dishes with the women as I usually do. As I stacked plates to carry into the kitchen the mother said, "No, Marcie, sit down. Don't work." The older brother, sitting at the table, interjected, "No, Mom, she's part of the family now. She is doing her part." The mother smiled reassuringly at me and said, "Now I have three daughters, Sharo, Eman and Marcie!" A broad smile spread across my face and my heart swelled with joy as I continued to "do my part" as a daughter and carried the dishes to the kitchen.

Cool breezes blew across us, fragrant orange blossoms perfumed the air, and the stars sparkled beautifully. Our voices and laughter lit up the night, and the love we exchanged in small glances, touches and sincere words surrounded us comfortingly. I reiterate what I said in the first week I spent with this family, "This is what I was born for." There are not words to adequately describe the satisfaction my heart experiences from being loved by them. The dream continues to come true.

I must leave in one week. Oh, how will I be able to leave this!

".....sorrowful, yet always rejoicing;

Poor, yet making many rich;

Having nothing, and yet possessing everything." (2 Corinthians 6:10 NIV)

Horizon

Story by Ellen

Ellen and her husband have lived in the Middle East for over five years. They have two young children. Ellen is a gifted poet and a caring and intuitive person. Here she tells of a young Muslim woman, Horizon, facing many problems in her life.

When I first met Horizon I sensed that she was different and that God really had a special purpose for her. Our friendship started as she became my language teacher. I felt I should start reading the Injil (New Testament) with her. She said, "I have never seen an Injil. Do you have one? What is the difference between the old and new part of the Bible?" That day she took home an Injil and told a mutual friend of ours, "I started reading the Injil today!" She seemed excited and willing to learn about Christ in the book of Luke.

As we began reading the Injil together she shared with me about her desire to know God more deeply but that her family wanted her to stay as she has been. She said, "Our family and community are very close. One could never think of marrying anyone outside of it. My parents want me to marry a man who is older than I and has money, but I don't really love him and I think he is boring, too!"

I have been able to visit Horizon's home and have met her family. They are very kind and hospitable but very cautious in any discussions of God or religion. Horizon, by contrast, is quite open about what she thinks about God and her relationship to Him. We have been studying different types of prayer, for forgiveness, for healing, and for help in time of need. She said she had a dream once where she felt God was telling her that He was there to help her and give her strength and that she needed to look to Him for direction in her life.

I am so grateful for Horizon. She is constantly keeping me on my spiritual toes to share truth in ways that have significance to her as a single woman. She said to me, "A woman is like a fragile vase; anything that touches her that shouldn't can bring a crack which everyone can see. I have to be so careful in any dealings with men outside of my family. It is almost too much at times." This culture brings great pressure and Horizon is constantly aware of the effect her actions could have on her family.

I wrote and dedicated the following poem to Horizon and other Muslim women who are seeking to know the Messiah, the lover of their souls.

Heart's Desire

We worship, we adore
the Everlasting Lord.
Eternal Truth and Life
we bow, we kneel
to our heart's desire.

Returning to the
fear of your ways,
we sense the gentle touch
of the Spirit's breeze,
calling us to pure worship.

Sustainer of our days
and Desire of our heart,
we quietly wait,
expectantly,
looking to you.

May we bring you pleasure,
May we bring you delight,
May we bring you gifts
from hearts full
of pure worship.

We worship, we adore
Thee, Everlasting Lord.
Eternal Truth and Life,
we bow, we kneel
to our heart's desire.

A horizon is something that is always ahead of you. Can you believe God to be that for Horizon, agreeing with me for her eyes to be always fixed on Jesus as the One who would continually be before her and fulfill her in every way? As I have thought of and prayed for Horizon, the following verse stands out to me for her. *"Whosoever offers praise glorifies me and to him who orders his conduct aright, I will show the salvation of God."* (Psalm 50:23 NKJV)

The "Evil Eye"

Story by Candice

Candice got an early start as an overseas worker. She first went to Central Asia at age 14 as a nanny to a Frontiers family. She was no stranger to the family, having been their baby sitter for several years prior to that trip. Her second trip was at age 17, at which time she developed a heart specifically for the women of that country. Now a college-age woman, Candice just returned from that country, where she got to know many women personally and hear some of their stories. One story about two women in particular is very encouraging and inspiring.

The people of my adopted country have many different idols, superstitions, and beliefs. One of their famous symbols for protection is called the "evil eye". The most common form looks like a blue eye and is on a pin that they wear in hopes that it will keep away evil spirits and give them protection. You can buy these blue eye pins everywhere. They're in every store. Some people do not even think about the implications of having them. But to some these objects are very powerful and they couldn't imagine not having them.

There is a family in a nearby village with whom our workers have become friends. The team has been able to share with this family how incredible and powerful Jesus is. The whole family is open to studying more about Him. A few of the women have become believers despite the rest of the family having not made this decision. These women are trying to live out the love of Jesus to the rest of the family so that they too might believe.

As these women are growing in their faith, they have become convicted of various sins or sin issues that need to be dealt with. One of these is their dependence on the evil eye for protection. For generations their people have depended on it for security, especially for their children. However, now these women have been told that Jesus is the ultimate protection and security, and He does not want us turning to an object to protect from evil spirits.

One day the women believers decided to act in obedience to this teaching and removed the evil eye placed on the baby of the household. When they tried to put the baby to sleep, she absolutely refused to go to sleep as she normally did. Instead she cried and cried. These cries turned into screams that would not stop. Everyone knew that there was something very wrong, that this was not her normal behavior. The old grandmother of the family was very afraid and attributed this outburst to having taken away the evil eye. She insisted that they put it back on the baby. The women were about ready to agree, but they knew that they had acted in obedience when they removed the eye. So they asked the grandmother to first allow them to pray over the baby in the name of Jesus. They essentially had only a minute to do so while the old grandmother ran off to fetch the eye pin.

They went over to the baby's crib and laid their hands on her and prayed for her in the name of Jesus. Immediately, the baby stopped crying! She calmed down and, to the amazement of all, drifted off to peaceful sleep, looking like a little angel! The whole family was able to witness how incredibly powerful the name of Jesus is! They are slowly being released from many fears that have held them in such bondage for a long time.

We rejoice that these two believing women had the courage and the spiritual strength to pray in Jesus' name in front of the whole family. My prayer is that they will be able to minister to their family and many of their friends in the future and continue to walk in obedience to the King.

"Come unto Me." (Matthew 11:28 KJV)

"Dreamer"

Story by Kim

Kim and her husband have worked in the Middle East for the past eight years, serving in two countries. They are a very gifted young couple and have three delightful children. This story of friendship evangelism will give you a glimpse of the spiritual battles being fought daily by our field workers. Kim and her associates befriended a Muslim woman whom God had given multiple spiritual dreams. Because of that, they dubbed the woman "Dreamer." She quickly came to faith but remained trapped in a life and death struggle in the occult. It was through the perseverance and prayers of Kim and her friends that Dreamer was finally freed from the occult and brought to full faith in Jesus Christ.

I met Dreamer in a very round-about way. Dreamer had started asking questions about Christian faith of a European woman, supposing she was Christian. However, this woman had converted to Islam in order to marry a Muslim man, and Dreamer's questions made her very uncomfortable. So she referred Dreamer to an Indian Christian woman who then referred Dreamer to her pastor's wife, who happened to be a friend of mine. It was this friend who asked me if I would be interested in trying to help Dreamer. I decided to ask a woman doctor friend to accompany me on my first visit to assess whether Dreamer was sincere. It was known that Dreamer had had problems in the past with schizophrenia. Also it was our standard practice to go in pairs. With that plan in mind we set up an appointment.

Dreamer seemed really pleased to have us in her home. She was an interesting but complicated woman. She was Arab, middle-aged, upper-class, single, and spoke fluent English. She was well educated, had traveled to Europe a number of times, and was accustomed to wearing western attire. She soon launched into telling us about twenty or more spiritual dreams she'd had over a 14-year period. As we listened, my doctor friend and I sat there amazed! For instance, in one of her dreams she saw a little lamb in someone's arms and heard the words, "This is the Lamb of God who takes away the sins of the world." In another she saw the "Last Supper" with Jesus and his disciples. In yet another, she saw a chunk of bread and an ancient looking chalice and heard a voice saying, "This is my body, take and eat; this is my blood, take and drink." She woke up horrified at the thought of what she had just heard, not understanding the context of it.

She told us that her interest in Christianity had started back in her college days when she went to a neighboring country with a college friend and visited an Orthodox church. She loved the liturgy, and a yearning for spiritual things was awakened in her. Unfortunately, since Christianity was not available to her, in her quest she turned to books on the occult, New Age, and mysticism.

Her Islamic family had no objection to her library of books on the occult as they viewed it as no threat to her belief or practice of Islam. She had five sisters who kept a very close eye on her, asking such questions as, "Are you a good Muslim? Do you pray five times a day?" If she spoke of her dreams, it would arouse suspicion from her family or co-workers. So she learned to be very discreet in her inquiries. One time she was desperate enough to find out what her dreams meant that she decided to take a risk and go to a secular video store to see if she could find anything on Christianity. She hoped that the clerk would not be Muslim, but Hindu, so as not to attract any undue attention. Thankfully, he was Hindu. She found a British film on the life of Jesus which really opened her eyes to the symbolism in her dreams.

After our first meeting with Dreamer, we knew she must be special to God or He wouldn't have invaded her life all those years with symbolic dreams and visions. So four of us women devised a plan to disciple her. We would go in pairs, twice a week, to meet with her. We would pray for and with her, share Scripture with her, give her literature to read, and help her in any way we could to come fully into the light and knowledge of the Gospel.

Dreamer readily embraced the Gospel. Her heart and mind had been prepared for this by her dreams and her spiritual quest. Yet, a great obstacle stood in her way. It was the practice of the occult which by now had a strong hold on her. She had relied on the teachings in her occult books for many years for guidance in her life. To her way of thinking, she could have both Christ and the occult. Our challenge was to convince her that it just couldn't work that way.

We set out to teach her that her mind and body were meant to be the temple of the Holy Ghost, that God was a jealous God who would not share her with any other gods or idols, that Christ has no fellowship with the devil, and that she would have to make a choice as to whom she would serve. We taught her that she must not have the slightest reliance on anything other than God. We read to her in Deuteronomy about the sinfulness of the occult and witchcraft. And we did a lot of praying.

A real struggle was going on in Dreamer's life. She suffered many things as she tried to "fix" her life her own way. She would have very bad, scary dreams and be terrified by them. She would feel the presence of evil in her apartment and call us in the middle of the night to pray for her. We explained to her that as long as she held onto the occult and kept possession of those books, she was inviting the enemy in and would not find the release she was seeking. We knew, of course, that only the Holy Spirit could do the real convincing. So we kept praying.

As we continued to work with her, not giving up on her, she became willing to release the books she had so long relied upon. It took three different "cleansing" times for her to give them all up. She also took her expensive charms and amulets to the second-hand shop, lamenting a little over the loss of money in the transaction. But she was relieved in knowing that she had done the right thing. As she began to release these things to God, He began to manifest His wonderful life in her! We could see Christ becoming visible in her life. She began reading the Bible regularly on her own. She got cable and found the 700 Club on European TV. She stopped smoking. She enjoys Christian music and plays it all the time. She loves to talk to people about the Lord and attends church regularly. She knows how much God loves her to give her those mysterious spiritual dreams and to send us to interpret them and to patiently guide her out of the dangerous pitfalls of the occult.

Looking back, I realize the great amount of energy and patience it took working with Dreamer. But I also know the great joy of seeing her come into the Light, having her questions answered, her soul satisfied, and her spirit set free!

"Let us not be weary in well doing for in due season we shall reap, if we faint not." (Galatians 6:9 KJV)

Jasmine: Ambitious Lady

Story by Donna

Donna has been on the field for eight years in Central Asia. She is a single woman, well educated and very capable in the business and social world. However, she left behind any aspirations these attributes might have brought her in order to answer a higher calling in the King's business which she loves.

I met Jasmine through a friend who had come to know her while working on a community aid project together. My friend, who was leaving the country, wanted me to follow-up with Jasmine. I said, "Sure, I'd love to meet her. She sounds like a great lady." And so she was!

Jasmine is an important person in her city in Central Asia. She is a "mover and shaker" among women in the work force and a very forward-thinking lady with visions of things she would like to do for the women of her country. Jasmine runs a women's association that helps the poor women in town. She also receives income from her radio and TV programs but not nearly enough to live on. Her husband is employed so they have a middle-class standard of living. Some of her ambitions are purely selfish, such as making herself more famous, more important. She often operates in the mode of, "It's all about me, my career and my reputation in town." Yet she is one of the few out front trying to make a difference and encourage the women of her country.

Jasmine must navigate some troubled political waters. Each political party in this country is like a military faction and she is trying to steer clear of them as best she can, not wanting to be part of any and yet not wanting to offend any.

Each political party has its own women's group that is endeavoring to pull Jasmine to its side. She must withstand a lot of criticism from all sides. As I've gotten to know her, I have come to appreciate what a strong, savvy, and energetic person she is. I do admire her a great deal for her initiative and for wanting to make a difference in her world.

One day as we got to know each other better, she inquired, "Donna, how do you Christians pray?"

I said, "Well, we just pray like we are talking. We just talk to God. We can pray right now if you want."

"Really?"

"Yes. Do you want to pray now?"

"Yes, let's pray," she agreed.

I put my hands out in Muslim fashion, palms up, and began to pray. I was trying to pray in her language, but I was not very fluent in it. Because Jasmine wanted to have a head covering on, as is their custom when women pray, she grabbed her prayer shawl and draped it over both of us. Suddenly we heard a crash! We looked up to see her three kids in a pile on the floor. Unknown to us they had been watching from the doorway and one of them, on roller skates, had slipped and pulled the rest down. When she finally got that commotion settled down, we prayed. I asked the Lord to show her beyond a doubt that God had heard her prayer.

About two days later she called me and excitedly said, "Donna, God heard! God heard my prayer!" Well, I was thinking that probably she'd had a dream or vision or some other spiritual breakthrough. But what she said was, "This (well known) British relief organization called me and told me they are giving me furniture for my office. They are giving me desks, files, chairs, couches and tables and much more!" It totally surprised me because in our prayer we never mentioned new furniture, but we did pray that God would bless her business. She was certain that this was a direct sign of God's answer to our prayer. After that she would often ask me to pray.

One day she came into my office all miserable and discouraged and told me of a bad situation in her office. Her superior at work had been sexually harassing her for some time. She knew that if she resisted him she could get fired. And if her husband found out about the harassment, he would literally kill the man. She said, "What am I going to do? We have got to pray." So again we prayed and the situation improved.

A few months later it was the International Women's Day, March 8th. Jasmine had gotten funding for a women's luncheon. She put together a lovely program: a kids' singing group and different speakers. I was there that day. All went well up to a point, but suddenly everything shattered. To the dismay of everyone present, one woman speaker started criticizing Islam from the platform while the video cameras were rolling! The woman refused to give up the mike and had to be forcefully removed. After that, every woman who took the platform felt she had to offer a rebuttal. People across that huge banquet hall were yelling and counter-yelling at each other. There was not even a pretense of decorum. It turned into a nightmare. Unfortunately, one woman called the local war-lord who controlled the TV station and told him that Jasmine brought this speaker up on stage to intentionally criticize Islam. That night she received a phone call saying she was fired!

When I visited her the next day, she was totally devastated and in the pit of depression. I feared she might try suicide so I stayed with her just to be there for her. She told me how much these people had hurt and betrayed her. I counseled her that she could not take revenge, that she had to forgive those who hurt her and let God handle this. I reminded her how much God had forgiven all of us and that she must, even for her own health's sake, forgive and go on. I told her that God wanted to heal her from all roots of bitterness and pain from the past that may be related. I encouraged her to just talk to God as we had prayed many times. I prayed that God would show her that He had not forgotten her and that somehow, out of this mess, good things would come.

Later God provided a means for her to be funded for the whole next year! He is using blessings on her professional work to demonstrate that He is there and is caring for her.

Through all this our friendship has grown. At times she will look at me and say, "You Christians are such good people. You are great, so nice and loving." I just keep answering, "We are just like anybody else except for the love of Jesus. It's not because we are good people. It's because of Jesus." Jasmine is not yet ready to align herself with Christianity, but she is moving forward, step by step. And I am encouraged and blessed to be a part of her life.

Rescued In A Dream

Story #2 by Donna

It is well known that Muslims are influenced by dreams and visions. God frequently works in this way to prepare hearts to receive His grace. Here are the events that led up to a memorable night in Donna's apartment when Galia accepted the Lord and dedicated herself to Christ, who changed her life completely.

Galia had moved from a very poor village into the city where I was living. She began working in a cotton factory where other villagers worked. All the village workers lived in dormitories provided for them, but their situation was almost like prison labor. Sometimes they would get paid and sometimes not. Sometimes they would receive material they were manufacturing in exchange for their labor instead of the cash they deserved. Sadly, Galia was raped in her dorm. She became very fearful and life was very difficult and stressful for her.

One night Galia had a terrifying dream. She dreamed that she was in a huge pond of putrid and murky water. People all about her were drowning in it. She began screaming for help when a man heard her cries and came to the edge of the pond, reached in and pulled her out! He sat down with her and started telling her about Isa (Jesus). When she woke up from her dream she was very disturbed by it and wondered what it all meant.

Later she remembered hearing about a man, Victor, in the factory who, everybody said, had become a Christian. She thought maybe this man would know what her dream meant. Finding him, she told him her horrifying dream. Victor was an evangelist and told her she needed to come to his cell group meeting that night where she would meet others who had chosen to follow Isa. And there she would find out the meaning of her dream.

Galia was too fearful to come to the meeting alone, so she asked several friends to go with her. That night the group was meeting in my apartment. Victor's brother, Ivan, was leading the meeting. The two brothers were amazing evangelists and were leading lots of Muslims to the Lord. Even though both brothers worked at the cotton factory where Galia worked, God had arranged it so that Galia had not yet met Ivan.

I was still in the kitchen preparing food for the guests when the door bell rang, and Ivan answered the door. Imagine Galia's surprise when she recognized him as the man in her dream who had pulled her out of that putrid pond! She turned a little pale, yet said nothing about the dream. She and her friends came in to the meeting, taking it all in: the fellowship, the food, the music. Ivan gave an anointed message, explaining the way of salvation. Now everything seemed perfectly clear to Galia. She knew that the rescuer represented Isa and the putrid pond was her sins. She understood that she needed to be saved from her sins. At the end of the meeting she accepted the Lord as her Savior. There was an immediate transformation in her life. However, it was not until sometime later that she told us about her strange dream and how God had prepared her heart to receive Him.

Galia went on to become one of the strongest women leaders in the whole fellowship and has won many women to the Lord. She has returned to her village and won most of her family to the Lord! God has blessed her with business opportunities so that she is able to live a stable life. But financial stability, which in times past may well have been a goal of hers, is not what motivates her today. God is stirring in her heart a vision of becoming a missionary to her people in Mongolia. She is not Mongolian, but many of her own nationality have migrated to that remote country. She wants to go there to tell them the Good News of the Gospel.

What an amazing transformation God has bestowed upon this once fearful young woman to make her the strong, confident woman of faith that she is today!

Emira: My Reluctant Friend

Story by Megan

Megan and her husband have served in the Middle East for fourteen years. They have two children. In the wealthy Arab country where they serve, it is very difficult for westerners to make friends, especially women with women since the women are seldom outside the home for any occasion. All shopping, even the grocery shopping, is done by the men! Opportunities for friendships are rare, except those arranged by God. Here is Megan's story of her reluctant friend.

Before I ever met Emira, she just knew she wanted nothing to do with me. After all, I was an American and, no doubt, she had heard many derogatory remarks about western women. And she, being a devout Muslim woman, would surely find nothing at all in common with me. Even though I had been coming to her home twice a week for over a month to teach her children English, I had never met Emira.

I had been in the country for awhile when Mr. Bekem approached me about teaching his children English. We worked out all the details and I went to their home to start the lessons. To my surprise, instead of the mother of the house greeting me as is the custom there, it was the maid who opened the gate and escorted me to the upstairs room where I was to teach the children. I would teach three of the four children for about twenty minutes each. Cookies and tea were always sent up to the room, but the mother never made an appearance. I was always escorted in and out of the house by the maid.

After I had been teaching the children for more than a month, I accidentally saw Emira, the mother, as I was coming down the stairs. Protocol then demanded that she speak to me and entertain me. She invited me into her sitting room and ordered the maid to bring in some refreshments, but she kept looking at her watch. After she had looked at the watch four or five times, I realized that a call to prayer had just gone off. Knowing that the call to prayer was a very strong compulsion which she found difficult to ignore, I said to her, "Don't you need to go pray?"

She said, "No. I will stay here and when we have finished talking, then I will go pray."

I said, "No. I think you need to go pray."

She, a bit agitated, said "No. You're my guest and I will stay here and visit with you and after you leave I will go pray."

Then I said, "Prayer is one of most important things in my life. And I think you need to go pray, and I promise you that I will sit here and wait for you until you are finished. Then we can continue our talk."

Reluctantly, she agreed and went into the other room. While she was praying, God must have touched her heart because when she returned, her attitude was totally different! She was very kind and gracious to me. Whatever God put into her heart, the change was astonishing! She started asking questions about people in the Bible. She asked, "Do you have David in your Bible? What about Moses? What does the Bible say about Moses?"

So I shared with her about that. Well, that broke the ice. From then on Emira would come and meet me and we would sit and talk. When our Easter holiday came, I gave each of her children an Easter basket filled with candy. The children loved that! I explained to her that giving the baskets was a tradition in our country. I also included in each basket a children's New Testament in Arabic and English. Before giving them to the children I had asked Emira's permission and told her I knew that in the Qur'an it said that one should read the Injil (New Testament). So she allowed me to give the New Testaments to the children. At the same time I offered her a copy of the Jesus video. However, she wasn't ready for that and gave it right back to me. I had to be happy that I had made a little inroad.

As our friendship progressed, I learned Emira was an excellent cook! Since I wanted to improve my ethnic cooking skills, we made an agreement that I would exchange the language lessons for some cooking lessons. This arrangement worked out very well. I would watch her cook and write everything down. I learned how to make some wonderful Arabic dishes!

After I had known Emira for about six months, there was a tragedy in her family. Her sister-in-law, who was about nine months pregnant, had gone into the hospital for emergency surgery and died on the operating table. The baby also died. This happened during Ramadan, the month of fasting. When I heard about it, around three in the afternoon, I immediately ran over to her house to offer my condolences. But it is not the custom to go to anyone's house to call at that time of day during Ramadan because everyone is usually asleep. Although I did disturb her nap, she was very touched that I would come right away when I heard about her sister-in-law's death. I grieved with her through that sorrow.

About six months later her favorite sister also died. This was a very, very hard time for her. I went with her to the matam, which is like a fellowship hall for her religious group. Women were beating themselves on the chest and wailing loudly in their grief. I sat there with her for several hours. Afterwards she said to me, "No one has ever loved me or treated me the way you do, outside of my own family. I feel like you are my sister now. You have been through so much with me and loved me through it all and you have loved my children." So our relationship continued to grow.

Then the time came for us to leave and move to a neighboring country. Four years passed and it wasn't until last year, the fifth year, that I got to go back to our old country and see Emira. When we met she was very excited and wanted to speak to me privately. She quickly took me into the other room and said, "I have to tell you something."

"What is it?" I asked.

She said, "I have seen *The Passion of the Christ!*"

I said, "Well, how did you see *The Passion of the Christ*? It's illegal here."

She said, "I know, I know. I got a pirated DVD. But I watched it! I watched it several times!"

I said, "And what did you think about it?"

With tears in her eyes, she said, "It did something to my heart! It did something to my heart!"

I knew the great risk she was taking just to watch this video, probably keeping it from her husband and children, too. But I had to say to her, "I think you should watch it again and again. Keep watching it and see what God says to you, see how He talks to your heart."

Later, I reflected on the journey of our friendship. At first, she wanted nothing to do with me at all. But God's plan over-ruled. From the day of our seemingly accidental meeting, she recognized my deep faith and also my consideration for her faith. And God changed her heart. Then it was through the cooking lessons that she had something to offer to me, and our friendship bonded. When tragedy came, I grieved with her and she received my love as the love of a sister.

Finally, the wonder of it all! Long after I had gone from her life, she sought out a pirated copy of *The Passion* and secretly watched it, not once, but several times. It's wonderful to see God continuing to work in her life.

Childhood Revisited

Story by Hannah

This is a story by a young woman who as a child lived with her family in the Middle East. She tells of her love for a childhood friend, Aveen, and how their friendship developed. Her story will give you insight into the mindset, customs and culture of this Muslim community. Hannah was a real Daybreaker, bringing Light to this Muslim family. She is now a young woman and is preparing to return to this country to renew old friendships and to continue serving God and the people there.

My family went to serve in a Middle Eastern country when I was nine years old. We were the first Americans our neighbors had ever seen. For that reason we were of great interest and curiosity to them, and all the kids swarmed our home and wanted to meet us.

That very first evening we were invited to our neighbors' home for dinner. At this home were two girls about my age. They looked quite strange to us with their funny pigtails, and we must have looked funny to them because they just couldn't stop giggling at us!

After dinner the children took us into another room to play games. They knew a little English, so we managed to communicate well enough to play simple games. From this beginning, these two girls became my best friends for the next five years, even when one of them moved across town.

One of the girls was Aveen. Aveen was over at my house all the time. She loved to play with our kitty. My mom would have us exercise together. Aveen liked to try new foods and wanted to eat everything I was eating. For the first time she tried ketchup, mustard, cereal, grilled cheese sandwiches, brown sugar, spaghetti and many other American foods. She thought some of our food was weird, especially spaghetti, and would laugh with delight at it. Then I would go to her house where up on the flat roof, big metal trays of tomato sauce were baking in the sun. I tried a taste of it even though it really wasn't ready to be eaten and didn't taste very good. She laughed at the funny faces I made at the taste of it. So we had a lot of fun together.

Once, when my family came back to America for a visit and then returned to the field, we found that Aveen and her family had moved. I was devastated! We eventually learned, by asking neighbors, where they had moved to. How happy Aveen and I were to see each other again! We both shed tears of joy! Our parents began to drive us to each other's homes every weekend so we could spend some time together.

Those were wonderful childhood years playing and sharing so much together. Sometimes we would talk about our faith. When we had sleepovers, she would see me reading my Bible before bedtime. I was learning to practice my devotions. She thought that was neat, that

I was a "faithful" person. Also she observed that we prayed before mealtimes, but found it a little amusing that we children always said the same memorized prayer. Sometimes she would mimic us, but we knew it was in fun and we never took offense.

Although Aveen is a Muslim, I've never seen her pray or wear a scarf on her head. She is a very good person, and I'm sure she believes in God, but she doesn't know Him. It is very interesting that when we left the country, when I was fourteen, Aveen wrote a letter to our family saying, "Please come back. We're going to miss you and these are the things we appreciated about you." In the letter she said, "We know that Jesus is very important to you. Thank you for teaching us to love Him through you." But I think she said that out of wanting to please us rather than through actual experience of knowing Jesus.

When my family and I came home to America, our friendship was interrupted for eight years. Last year I was privileged to again visit that country on a short-term mission. When I saw my dear childhood friend, we hugged for a long time.

I found that much was happening in Aveen's life. She was now engaged to be married to her cousin! From childhood her family had committed her to this marriage. Such alliances are very common in that part of the country. As a result of these inter-related marriages, newborns are often deformed or have other genetic difficulties. In fact, I had known and seen two siblings of the cousin she was to marry who suffered birth defects. When I asked Aveen if she was worried about this, she said she cried whenever she thought of it but was still willing to take the risk because the marriage had been arranged. Even though her family will say it is Aveen's decision to marry her cousin, it is really a group decision. It is not her decision alone. In their eyes she is fated to carry on the family tradition.

However, some good things were happening for Aveen. She got a degree from a technical school and was working at a junior college as an accountant. She has her own pick-up which we drove all over town last summer. Her family is so proud of her because she is the first young woman in town to own a car.

I am going back to that country for one year, starting this summer, and I'm looking forward to continuing our friendship. God has put a great love in my heart for this people group. I pray to live out the words that Aveen spoke years ago. "We know that Jesus is very important to you. Thank you for teaching us to love Him through you." My prayer is that I will be the Message.

"You have been raised on the Message of the faith and have followed sound teaching. Now pass on this counsel to the Christians there, and you'll be a good servant of Jesus." (I Tim. 4:12 The Message)

The Story Of Joy

Story by Linda

Linda and her husband moved to a Middle Eastern country sixteen years ago with a one-year-old, a three-year-old and a five-year-old-all girls. Linda's husband died of cancer, yet she chose to remain and serve in that country. God has given Linda a unique ministry to women, partly because she is single and only has daughters. Two of her daughters are now grown and away at university while the third is still in high school and remains at home. These next three stories are contributed by her and show both the triumph and tragedy of the missionary life.

Joy was born in the Middle Eastern country where I am serving. As a young student she went to England to live with her aunt and uncle. All went well for a few years until her aunt and uncle learned that Joy, a Muslim, had become a believer in Christ. They immediately kicked her out of their house with literally nowhere to go. She walked into a church and there met a young couple who took her in.

Joy eventually got a job in the tourism industry as a tour guide, taking groups to her native country in the summertime. By now life had become very settled for her in England, and her plans were to remain there for the rest of her life. But she began to sense that God was saying, "Go back to your home country because I need people there who will be as light in the darkness. Your country is still such a dark, dark place." At first she resisted because when her parents found out through her uncle that she had become a Christian, they wrote to her and told her not to even think of coming back home to live as a Christian. They said, "You are a Muslim! You were born a Muslim and that can never change." Joy knew that her family would never, ever, accept her new faith.

But the conviction grew in her heart that God wanted her to return to her own country. When she would lead the tours in the summers, and come to our little church, she got encouragement through us and our pastor. So Joy decided to move back and let go of her good job in England. Oddly enough, her family received her back into their home, probably hoping that she would forget this new religious faith that she was involved in. Then, too, in that culture it was only proper that a single lady live with her family.

Joy started coming to our little fellowship and to the cell group which met in my home. I began meeting with her regularly, and it soon became apparent that she was going through some deep culture shock. She started thinking that coming home had been a mistake, that she didn't like it here, and that she was not of this culture anymore because of the many years she had spent in England. She considered that in England there were men she might marry, but here there was nobody. She was very discouraged. However, I could see that Joy had great potential to bring the Gospel to people in her own culture. I counseled her and basically persuaded her to stay. Of course, we put the matter before the Lord in prayer.

Joy needed a job because her parents insisted that she support herself. Many job offers started coming in, but they would have pulled her away from the church and its community. For that reason she felt those jobs were not right for her. She started praying, "Lord, give me a job that will let me work right here in this community, and let me be a part of this very small group." The Lord did open a door for her and gave her a very good job right here. She stayed and kept becoming more and more involved in the church.

So it went for a year. I was so glad because we desperately needed nationals who had a heart for their own people. I felt that this was what the Lord really wanted for her. Joy was a great encouragement to me and others. During this year my husband became ill and went through his battle with cancer and died. I was continuing with the cell group ministry, and she was very much a part of that group. As another year went by, we were growing very close in our work together.

One Sunday morning the police invaded our church service and all forty of us were arrested and hauled off to jail. We were kept in prison for 24 hours. We were treated as if we were terrorists. It was a very difficult time. When we were arrested, a lot of news photographers were there taking pictures because the police had notified the newspaper in advance. So our arrests became a big media event. We were on the evening news and the morning news. Our pictures were in the newspaper, with the most prominent picture being of Joy's arrest. Of course, her family and neighbors saw those pictures.

We were all released the next day. But when Joy went home, she went to a silent home. Her family thought at first, "Well, maybe no one will notice." But soon it became apparent that the whole neighborhood had heard about their daughter. And this, of course, was a huge shame to them. The son who lived in the same building forced the family to take action when he came home in a rage, threw open the door and said, "Is Joy here?"

They said, "Yes, she has come back, she is here."

The son said, "I am going to kill her myself if you do not throw her out this instant! She has brought great shame on us all. She must not be a part of this family anymore."

He was so wrathful and full of rage that in order to protect her from him, the family told her to get out. I'll never forget hearing a knock at my door late that night and, upon opening it, finding Joy there with her suitcase in hand, tears streaming down her face, telling me her family had kicked her out. I took her into my arms and said, "Well, you've always got a home here."

There was already another woman in our home who had been kicked out of her home because of the arrest. The two of them stayed with us for the next four months. I was able to do this because we were all women in the house. I had two daughters still at home. I had no sons and I was a widow. That made a very convenient home for taking in women. Joy's family wouldn't speak to her during those four months.

There was one very good thing that came out of that arrest. For some time Joy had been secretly dating a young man in our church. That ill-fated day of the arrest was the day they had previously chosen to sit together in church, thereby announcing to the people that they were in an official dating relationship. So the arrest actually turned out to be rather great for them because instead of having just the Sunday morning together they had the next 24 hours together! We all noticed how kind and considerate he was of her, trying to protect and take care of her. Over the next few months while she was living in my home, their relationship continued to grow, which would not have been very easy had she been living at home.

Her parents heard that she was planning to marry a Christian man. Even though they did not want her to marry a Christian, they insisted that she come back home and leave her family home as a bride, this being a very strong family tradition. I was a bit fearful for her to do this, not really knowing to what lengths they might go to prevent the marriage, but Joy, being a very loving and forgiving person, went back home as her family had requested. Now resigned to this marriage, her parents arranged a civil ceremony which they and other family members could attend. When that was done, Joy came back to my home, waiting several days before she and the young man were formally married in the church with all her Christian friends in attendance.

Their family loves them and has welcomed them back into their homes, but the family themselves have not turned to the Lord. Joy and her husband are happy in their marriage and ministry and full of hope for the future.

Latifa: Demon Possessed

Story #2 by Linda

Ibrahim, a former Muslim, now a believer, came to us and said, "You know, I have a new neighbor in my apartment building and I am very distressed about her. Her name is Latifa. My neighbor keeps coming to me, saying he does not know what to do for his sister, because she is continually trying to commit suicide. They always have to keep someone with her to protect her. She is a young woman with two children. She is always trying to jump off balconies. And once she tried to hang herself. She has been driven to do this by demons. I feel I need to help her, to do something for her. Would you go with me to pray for this woman?"

My husband said, "If her family is willing, of course, we would be willing to help." So Ibrahim, accompanied by my husband, went to the family and told them he was a believer in Jesus Christ. This was a big risk for him, but he really wanted to help this family. He told them we would love to pray for their sister in the name of Jesus Christ for her to be healed and delivered from this terrible bondage.

We learned that this woman had been under attack for more than ten years. Her family had taken her to every witch doctor they could think of. In fact, they had taken her all over the country trying to find someone who could help. They understood this was a spiritual problem. No one was able to help her. And they were desperate because not only was she in danger but it was a very great strain for everyone in the family.

It is typical in the Middle East for the whole family to live in the same building. The parents live on one floor, and as the children grow up and get married they just move onto the next floor. There were five floors in this building, and all the floors were occupied by family members. Latifa and her family lived on the ground floor simply because it was too dangerous for her to be anywhere higher.

The family agreed to allow us to come and pray for Latifa. We told them we first must share with them why we pray in the name of Jesus and who He is. They agreed to that as well. Because I was a woman, I was allowed every day for a week to speak with Latifa and her sister and Latifa's husband. I read Scripture with them to show them who Jesus is and why we believe that only Jesus Christ has the power to heal and to free her from this kind of demonic bondage. They were very open. There were a few times, however, when Latifa would become violent and the men would have to hold her down.

But the family and Latifa, when she was in her right mind, were very positive and would say, "Yes, please, please help us." We set a date for about a week later and started fasting and praying. When that date arrived, we took Latifa and her husband and her sister to our little church, which was actually an apartment on the bottom two floors of a building. We gathered together, Latifa and her family, my husband and I, and our pastor. For about three hours we worshiped and then began casting out demons from her by taking authority over them in the name of Jesus Christ. The power of God worked very mightily and forcefully and when we finished, Latifa was like a different person! There was such peace written on her face, and her family was amazed. They said, "Wow! We haven't seen her looking like this for a long time."

Then we had some refreshments. Our pastor talked with her and her family and her husband and said, "Now you can see that the true power is in Jesus Christ. And He is the one who can set you free. Are you ready to put your faith in Him, your trust in Him?" They conferred a while between themselves and they turned to us and said, "You know we love Jesus. We can see He is more powerful than anybody else. We can see this is true. But we could never, ever, leave Mohammed. We could never turn our backs on Mohammed." And that was their final decision that night. Of course, this was very discouraging to us because we had hoped that when they saw the power and the truth of the Gospel that they would bend the knee to Jesus Christ, but they said, "No." We saw we couldn't persuade them, and so we left it at that. We said, "This is your decision. You have seen the Truth and you have seen it in a very powerful and living way. We will continue to pray for you, but you have made your choice here this night." And they left.

About a week later all the women of the family came to visit me. They were so elated over Latifa's recovery and so grateful for what we had done. They said, "This is the first time in years we can leave her alone. She is like a different person. She is able to be the mother she always wanted to be. The children are no longer having nightmares at night." But during the time we were all having tea, Latifa came to me and asked if she could speak to me privately. We went into the back bedroom and she said, "You know, I'm starting to hear voices again and sense that things are just going to start happening again." And I said, "Latifa, I cannot help you if you do not bend the knee to Jesus Christ and acknowledge Him as your Savior, because it is only in His Name that you can stand up against the evil forces." And she said, "I cannot do that." I told her I would pray for her but the choice was hers. I realized she was just not strong enough to stand against the family's group decision.

After another week went by, the family asked all of us who had been involved with Latifa that night to come to their home where they wanted to honor us with a feast.

There were seven of us believers, and from Latifa's family there were about 15 to 20 people. On the terrace, which was on the roof of their five-story house, was a large table setting. After an elaborate meal, we were just starting tea time when I noticed Latifa was missing. I asked about her and her sister-in-law said that Latifa had complained of being a little tired and had gone to lie down in one of the rooms off the terrace. "But," she continued, "Latifa is fine. We don't have to watch her anymore like we used to."

As this conversation was going on, we were suddenly interrupted by sounds of horrific screaming and screeching! We realized that something terribly wrong was happening. People were shouting and crying out from below. In one instant the atmosphere of peace and joy was rent apart, and this family who had suffered so much was thrown into hysteria and panic. Adults were tipping over tables as they jumped to their feet, and children were running everywhere. Others were trying to get down the narrow staircase to get to the street level. The lights weren't working! Pandemonium had broken out!

When Latifa had excused herself to go in and lie down, she had actually been taken over by evil spirits and had crawled out the window on the fifth floor. She was standing on a ledge overlooking the street, screaming at the top of her lungs that she was going to jump and take her life. Of course, all the neighbors were screaming at her not to jump. Latifa's children were in hysterics and I was trying to comfort them. One of the sisters-in-law had a panic attack and couldn't speak.

My husband and another man, a believer, were at the window where Latifa had climbed out onto the ledge. Her husband was climbing out trying to get her back in. Her father, however, was in such a rage against her that he just wanted to push her off the balcony and be done with it. As soon as they got her back in the building, her father attacked her and beat her wildly and the men had to intervene and hold him back. The mother had a heart attack and an ambulance was called. The police were also called by the neighbors. They said, "We have just had enough. Get this family out of the neighborhood because this is happening all the time."

It took three hours to calm everything down. It was Satan's heyday. We felt sorry for poor Latifa, who had to be institutionalized. We, of course, understood that the defeat was because of the choices

Leila: Devout Muslim Friend

Story #3 by Linda

Leila is a close Muslim friend of mine. She was my first friend when I moved into this neighborhood 13 years ago, and we quickly became very close. She was quite a conservative Muslim, wearing a head covering and very devout. We were often in each other's homes. She had three girls and I had three girls who were near the same ages. In our neighborhood the children played in the streets because nobody had yards. Leila and I would sit and watch the children play. Often we would prepare food together and visit our neighbors together. My family and I were the only foreigners in the neighborhood because it was what might be called "the other side of the tracks." So no foreigner ever lived there. My husband and I felt that the Lord was calling us to live among the poor because it was mostly people from those kinds of neighborhoods who were coming to the Lord.

One day when we were talking, Leila told me that she was sure that nobody of her religion or nationality would ever become a Christian. To her, as to most Muslims, their religion is synonymous with their nationality. She went on to say that it was just impossible, and unheard of, for anybody to change their religion. I said, "Well, no, I know people of your nationality who have become believers in Jesus Christ." But she refused to believe that. She said, "No! It's unheard of, it's impossible." At that time she did not know that her own husband had become a believer!

A few days later I invited two women who were in the local fellowship to come to my home, and I invited Leila over to meet them. I said, "Well, here they are–living examples. You see, it is possible to be of this nationality and to be a believer in Jesus Christ." Her question to them was, "Well, you must not be truly of this nationality. Your mother must have come from outside the country or somewhere else. Surely you can't be pure nationals."

And they answered, "Yes we are. We come from Muslim homes and Muslim backgrounds." Then they proceeded to give her their testimonies. That was quite a shock for Leila and quite a paradigm shift for her. She had to really think through all that she had thought before.

Although her husband, Ibrahim, had become a believer, he kept it from Leila for awhile. We encouraged him to be open and tell her, but he struggled with that because he knew she was so dead set against it. He had become part of a fellowship that met each week in our home. We were becoming more and more his family, his spiritual family. Leila saw this happening, but she was in denial. She figured he was just curious, that he just wanted to find out what it was all about. She could not bring herself to accept that he actually had become a believer.

After a year he was baptized secretly without telling her. We had been encouraging him to tell his wife, and we thought she knew, but he had kept it a secret from her. A week later, late at night, we heard a knock on our front door. There they were–she had found out about his baptism. We invited them in, and for an hour she ranted and raved. She was furious with him and said to him in front of us, "You know, I could take anything. I wish you had been an adulterer, I wish that you had been a murderer, gone to jail, lost your reputation, or lost your job. This is the worst thing you could ever do. You will burn in hell, you will never be forgiven. You have turned apostate against your religion." She was so very upset. She said this was the biggest shame that had ever come upon them. And she wanted to make sure nobody ever found out. She ranted on, "What if my family hears? What if your family hears of this? I can't believe this is happening!"

It was very difficult for us because we could not comfort her in the way she wanted us to since we didn't agree with her. We encouraged her to wait and see if he changed and what this new found faith did in his life.

It has now been ten years since that day, and a lot has gone on. Ibrahim did remain faithful to the Lord. He had some difficult years, especially when my husband, his best friend, died. For several years he did not come and meet with us regularly. But then he came back and God did some wonderful healing in his life. He changed. He changed as a husband and as a father. Leila acknowledged this. She said, "Yes, he has become a better person in every way." She grew to know the other believers. She became a familiar part of our church gatherings. Sometimes she would join Ibrahim when he would come Friday evenings to our home for our cell group meetings. At times she would allow the children to come, but she would never acknowledge Christ. She always insisted, "I will never ever leave Islam. I will never do what he has done. I will not become apostate." And she has held that view to this day.

Two years ago, Ibrahim, who had taken up cigarette smoking as a teenager, developed lung cancer, and within five months he died. It was very hard for Leila. She loved him dearly, and they actually had a very good marriage. Two nights before he died, she walked with me in the garden of the hospital and said to me, "You know, I have come to the place of realizing that maybe Christians will go to heaven, both Christians and Muslims." So I could see that she at least had come far enough to recognize that her husband, as she put it, would be forgiven for what he had done. She could even see that this was the will of God, that there was some truth in this.

It's been hard for Leila since her husband's death. His family turned on her and accused her of not trying hard enough to prevent him from becoming a Christian. They said it was her fault! And in her pain, it's me she shares with, because she can't share with anybody else. She carries a heavy burden. I have said to her, "If you would trust in the Lord Jesus Christ this wouldn't be such a heavy burden, and you would find joy in it." She has heard a lot of the Gospel. She has seen the Jesus film. Her husband had talked with her over the years but neither she nor her three daughters, who are now grown, have ever made a decision to believe in the Lord Jesus Christ.

I continue to meet with her regularly. I have breakfast with her every other week, and after we have our tea I read to her the Gospel of Luke, while she does her tatting. We are still praying for Leila and are still very much involved in her life.

Ramadan In Africa

Story by Vickie

Vickie and her husband and three children have lived in Africa only a short while. She is a registered nurse by profession. She says, "When God called our family to leave America we were at a comfortable position in our lives financially, socially and professionally. We love it here but fight with culture shock and homesickness." Vickie gives you a wonderful glimpse into their lives and brings you right into Ramadan with them.

Ramadan is a Muslim's highest holiday. Fasting during Ramadan is one of the "five pillars of the faith," and Muslims take it very seriously. It is meant to be a time of purity and prayer, reflecting on God. People fast from sunrise to sunset. At the first sign of nightfall the fast is broken with a large family feast. In many respects, it seems more like a month of feasting, rather than fasting. They do this for 29 days!

In our home we hear, VERY LOUDLY, the call to prayer five times a day. About three more times a day we hear chants and Qur'anic verses. This is all broadcast from a loud speaker on the mosque's minaret and it echoes throughout the neighborhood. Each neighborhood has its own mosque and its own call.

At the breaking of the fast each night, a cannon goes off to let everyone know that it is time to eat and okay to smoke. The entire city stops, and the only thing you can hear is the sound of families eating a meal together. We often stand on our front porch and listen to the clattering of dishes and forks and moving chairs around the table. The streets at this time of day, which moments before were full of people and cars, are empty for about two hours. It feels like a ghost town and is a little spooky.

The practice of Ramadan brings family togetherness, cultural unity, and a move towards being more religious and spiritual. However, to say that people do not extend grace to each other during the daytime is putting it lightly! Fasting tends to make everyone mean and agitated. It is hard to make plans as things open late and close early each day. NEVER try to catch a taxi around 5:00 p.m. It can't be done!

Not everything about Ramadan is hard for us. Tonight we were invited to break the fast (they call it shockun fotter) with our house-cleaning lady, Sammy, whom I am really getting to know and love. She invited our family and one other American family that knows her well. She is very poor, but she fed us an amazing meal. She served five different dishes, each of which took a long time to prepare. Their house is open to the outside in some places. She has four children who live with her (three are grown) and they all sleep in the same room. Her kitchen is just a tiny room with a small fridge and no cabinets, no countertops, no table, and no stovetop or oven. She prepared the entire meal while kneeling on the floor with the same kind of little propane stove that we use for camping in the States. The food was amazing! She did all this with grace and style, and we all had a great time. I brought a cake and Sammy taught me some traditional dishes.

The Lord is daily increasing love in my heart for Sammy. She is part of a larger family to whom our group is reaching out. Sammy's sister, Remie, is a follower of Jesus. Just the other day I was feeling very homesick and spending time with my English-speaking friends, sharing my struggles with them. Remie was in the room and prayed for me, through tears, in her native tongue. It was the most beautiful prayer that I have ever heard, yet not understood. My friends translated for me. She had boldness and confidence to lift me to our loving Father. (It encouraged me that others like her will come to Him in that way, soon.) We both held each other and cried. It was so beautiful. Remie and I are sisters in Christ! My heart longs for her actual blood sister, Sammy, to know the loving arms of Jesus wrapped around her.

In a recent prayer letter to friends, I mentioned that yes, it is hard here and yes, I am homesick. Yes, I hate the heat and the difficulties of life without a car and not knowing much of the language. But I am finding that moments like these eclipse all of it when I consider what God is doing in my life and the lives of others. God brought us here to complete a work in us just as much as He brought us here to do a work for Him. He is fashioning us to be more like Him and it is hard work, but well worth it. I want to be more like Jesus, and I have a long way to go. But praise God, He's not finished with any of us yet!

Going On The Hajj

Story by Karen

Karen is a young single woman serving in South East Asia. Her trusted assistant, Leta, had stolen a rather large sum of money from her. This story shows what interpersonal relationships with nationals can be like on the field. It also reveals how Karen graciously, but firmly, handled the situation.

Note: "Going on the Hajj" means taking a trip to Mecca, the most holy site for Muslims. This is one of the five required duties of Islam and the trip must be made at least once in a person's lifetime.

After I got back from furlough in the U.S., I found out that my dear assistant, Leta, was not incapable of betraying a trust I had in her. When I asked her where the bank book for our credit project was, she said she didn't want me to see it. I'm no rocket scientist, but from that I concluded there might be a problem. Finally, she showed it to me, giving me a lengthy explanation of why there was almost $1,000 missing.

In my absence, after she had returned from the Hajj, she and her companion were absolutely penniless. They had used everything they had to go on the Hajj, along with money they had been given by people to buy souvenirs which they were expected to bring home to family and friends. They had nothing. That is why Leta had to "borrow" from the credit project to pay electricity bills, water bills, regular household bills, and telephone bills (that the neighbor girls had run up sky high). In addition, she'd wanted her mother to come and visit from a city miles away. Along with the mother, Leta's sister and some of her children wanted to come. So, Leta paid for them all!

I was feeling sick as she was telling me this, but not nearly as sick as she was in having to "fess up." I could tell it pained her to have to tell me. To her credit, she had listed out every single dollar that she had "borrowed" and was able to account for nearly everything that she spent. Also to her credit, after she finished explaining all this to me, she handed me about $750, the proceeds of selling her motorcycle, to start the repayment process. She had already sold it! She told me she would pay the remaining amount back in installments. I'm going to let her, of course. I know that she needed money, but I also know that Leta loves to give and when it came to her mother, sister, and the children, the sky is the limit. Now she's regretting her generosity.

I find it interesting, the timing of this error in judgment on Leta's part. She had just gotten back from her obligatory "religious performance" of a lifetime and stepped off the bus right into deceit– proof once again that if we're relying on "performance" to get us through, we will never get there–never. So, I'm praying for Leta to be broken about this, broken to the point of wondering why and how this could happen, especially after she had gone to all the trouble and expense to "fix herself" and supposedly be in such a "pure standing" before God. This was my prayer before the Hajj and still is: "Lord, let this be the biggest 'let down' she has ever experienced. Let her seek Truth."

A Day In The Life Of Bonnie

Story by Bonnie

Bonnie is a young single woman serving in a village in Africa. She has remarkably adapted to a culture so different from her own and finds joy in her mission. Her story is rich in "local color" and will show what a typical day in the village is like for her. Enjoy!

MARIANA!!! MARIANA!!! UMU JUULA WEETI! UMU JUULA WEETI!" It's the voice of my village mom, waking up the first of her oldest son's two wives. Today it's her turn to make breakfast, and everyone in our household groans and turns over as they try to ignore this unwelcome wake-up call. It is about 6:15 in the morning, but no one knows that because no one tells time here. About an hour ago, the silent darkness was pierced by the local imam's voice, "Allahu Akbar." That and the now fading starlight tell us that it is morning.

My village family owns a cluster of four mud houses. We all spent the night scattered over the ground in the center of the compound. Before rising I must cover my hair with a head scarf. My hand searches around in the darkness for it. After covering my head, I put my bedding back in the house and then take a little blue teapot outside and wash my face. This must be done in the presence of all, as you're not officially awake until you've washed your face, and you cannot speak to anyone until it's done. After that I take a walk with the Lord out in the bush. It wasn't until after I had lived with my family for several months that I discovered that "I'm going for a walk in the bush" means "Nature's calling and I'm going out in the bush to take care of business." Now they know that I'm going out there to pray.

When I return from my walk, I join my 25 family members under a thatch covering in the middle of our compound. It's there that we eat breakfast and lunch and spend all of our time during the day. Every day breakfast is a piece of bread and a steaming cup of kinkiliba, which is a local beverage made from cooked leaves that must be drowned in sugar in order to be edible. At least they think so. After the morning breakfast hour, the adults lie down under the thatch trying to catch a bit more sleep while the kids run around yelling and screaming and hitting each other, making quite a ruckus. Every morning my village mom washes the newborn babies of the family. (Yes, there are always plenty of newborns to be washed.) When everyone has finished eating, I collect the dishes and wash them. Then I change into my street clothing–a scarf and outer flowing garment–before heading off for our development project office.

Three mornings a week our team meets together to pray for our region and our adopted people. After prayer, I spend the morning in my oven of an office, working on e-mails and other office projects and activities. At 1:00 we have our daily lunch of fish and rice. We all sit around one common bowl, creating balls of food which we eat with our right hands. (Touching food with the left hand is strictly prohibited.)

At 1:30 in the afternoon I leave the office for my language helper's house. It's the hottest part of the day, and sometimes the skin on my flip-flopped feet hurts just to be exposed to the sun. I walk down the trash-cluttered dirt roads, dodging donkey carts, goats, and chickens, and also fish guts that have been thrown onto the road by women preparing lunch.

At the home of my language helper, Daniela, I'm bombarded by a slew of kids yelling my name and asking me for the 100th time to take their picture. I walk into each of the houses in Daniela's compound and make sure that I thoroughly greet ALL of the women in her family: "How are you? How have you spent the morning? How's the fatigue? How's the heat? How is your family? How are your kids? Are they in good health?" These are just some of the required greetings. I then sit down with Daniela for my language lesson. About 15 minutes into the lesson, I think I've lost a liter of sweat and wonder if I can focus on another hour's worth of language learning. However, with Daniela the time seems to pass quickly as we enjoy talking together in the local language about the culture and customs of the people of that region.

Late in the afternoon, when it has cooled down a little (relatively speaking), I take a walk to one of my national friend's houses. My visits to Margaret always begin with the series of ritual greetings. After that I sit down under her thatch and wait for her while she does her regular prayers right in front of me. She then sends one of her little girls to the local corner shop to buy sugar and powdered milk, which she uses to make me tuffam, the favorite drink of this people group. Sitting together on the ground, we enjoy tuffam and peanuts and conversation. After an hour or two, Margaret will walk me part of the way home.

I try to arrive home before dusk. That means that my shower can be taken without the nuisance of cockroaches that call our "bathroom" home. Our bathroom consists of a hole in the ground surrounded by a mud wall. It is there in the evenings that I take my bucket of water and "shower."

My evenings at home are spent picking up children and whirling them around, to their great delight, or sitting with the new bride as she prepares the evening meal, or watching our 15 kids try to round up all of the goats, sheep, and donkeys for the night. It's quite a sight!

Nightfall is marked by another call from the local mosque. In response, all of the adults in my family, along with some kids, bow down to the east in prayer. Once night falls, I collapse on the mat next to my village mom. As I sit with her, I hope that my prayers that day for ability in the local language and creativity for conversations will be answered. Then I'll go sit with Juliana, my village sister and closest friend, and enjoy conversation and laughter with her (one of my favorite times), before we're called for our daily dinner of sandy grain and runny green sauce.

Later in the evening, we'll all pull our bedding out into the middle of the compound again. Not long after we've all fallen asleep, we'll likely be wakened by quarrelling donkeys about to trample us in the heat of their fighting, or by restless sheep, or by Sahara wind strong enough to carry us all away. If we're lucky, we'll sleep until the next morning, when again we'll hear my village mom calling, "MARIANA!!! MARIANA!!! UMU JUULA WEETI!"

Naheed Has A Fairy

Story by Jane

Jane was new to the field, serving with her husband in South East Asia. She was totally unprepared for, and baffled by, a neighbor's sister who "had a fairy." Here is Jane's intriguing story!

During one summer we lived downstairs from Shaneen and her family. I became very well acquainted with all of them. On one occasion when I was visiting Shaneen, her sister, Naheed, came over. Naheed was a single woman, still living with her mother and father and brothers. The first thing I noticed was that there seemed to be some atmosphere of embarrassment or secret about her in her interaction with her family. A lot of joking or secret laughter was going on, especially among Shaneen's daughters. At first I thought this might be all directed at me, being a foreigner who didn't understand all their cultural ways. But I soon realized there was something more.

Shaneen's daughters kept laughing and bothering their mother, asking, "Mother shall we tell her?" And Shaneen would answer, "No, no. We are not going to talk about that." But eventually they did start talking about it. Their secret was that Naheed had a fairy! That is just how they said it. Naheed had a fairy that would come upon her from time to time. At first I thought they were just joking about this. But eventually they did convince me that Naheed really did have a fairy who would visit her and interact with her and actually directed her life.

I asked Naheed, "When does the fairy come to see you? How do you know the fairy is there?" She answered, "I see the fairy all the time. Sometimes I see her flying on the balcony. Other times she comes and sits on my shoulder, and that is when she takes over my body and speaks through me. She is very small with fairy wings so she can fly about. She has blond hair and blue eyes and always wears very beautiful clothing. She lives in the village in a fairy house with her fairy family."

When I asked Naheed how she got the fairy (or the fairy got her) she said it had just come upon her one time and has been with her ever since. She felt that having the fairy gave her prestige and honor in her family and community and made her feel special.

This was something I had never come across. When I went home, I told my husband about it. We knew that people in that culture used charms and amulets and believed in saints and prayed at their tombs. These things were common. But to actually meet somebody who had communication and daily interaction with a demonic spirit was very disturbing. We decided to make it a focus of prayer, especially prayer for my protection as I interacted with this family.

The next time I saw Naheed was at her own house where she lived with her mother and father and her brothers. I had come with Shaneen for a visit. Unexpectedly that afternoon, I witnessed the "take over" of Naheed by the fairy. Suddenly the room became very quiet, and someone said, "Oh, oh. The fairy is coming." Of course, I didn't see the fairy, nor did anyone but Naheed. I saw Naheed wave her arms in the air, then bring her arms down over her face in a crisscross fashion. Her demeanor and voice changed slightly.

Then the other family members proceeded to have a conversation with the fairy, who spoke through Naheed. It sounded like they were having a business meeting. While this was going on, the fairy gave Naheed words to write down to sell as amulets and charms to people. The meeting was actually getting quite animated with the mother arguing with the fairy, who was still speaking through Naheed. They were talking about money and prices. After the argument on prices, they discussed the best way to sell the amulets and charms Naheed had just produced. The conversation went on for about half an hour. Then Naheed raised her arms over her face again, gave a deep sigh, closed her eyes and said, "Okay, she left."

When they showed me the paper that Naheed wrote under the guidance of the fairy, it just looked like scribbles on the page. However, Naheed, who was totally illiterate, said that she could fully interpret the signs and that each had a specific power and meaning. Some of them were for protection from the "evil eye," some for fertility, some for healings and other things.

The fairy seems to be in complete control of Naheed's life. Although Naheed is a single woman well into marriageable age in that culture, she told me that it is up to the fairy whether or not she can ever marry. We could see that the fairy was providing a means of income for the family and that they wished that to continue.

As we were praying for this family, the story of Paul and the slave girl came to mind. How angry her owners became because they lost their source of income when Paul cast out the demon in her. We also thought about how sly and cunning Satan is to mask his appearance as a beautiful little fairy creature with a child-like appearance to gain complete control over this family.

At that time we did not feel led to confront the evil spirit in Naheed. We continue to be friends with this family and pray for their deliverance from demonic control. Our prayer is that God would reveal Himself to them in all His glory, that He would liberate them and set them free.

"If the Son sets you free, you shall be free indeed." (John 3:36 NIV)

Arranged Marriage In India

Story by Ingrid

Ingrid is a nurse and is a single woman. She has lived in India for four years. Here she relates a story about her special relationship with Shapira, her language helper and good friend. Shapira was very anxious about her forthcoming arranged marriage to a man she had never met. Through their friendship Ingrid was able to comfort and pray for Shapira. This story also gives us a great insider view of a Muslim wedding ceremony.

My prayer before I went to India was, "Lord, please give me a special friend on the field, a friend who can help me learn the language." The second week I was there, a teammate and I were out walking when we met some women from the village. They started a conversation with us and invited us to their house for tea. They were a very nice, friendly family. One of the daughters, Shapira, a teacher, agreed to give me some language lessons. From then on I went to her house twice a week and got to know the whole family and was graciously accepted by them.

After I had known them for awhile, I learned that Shapira was soon to be married. She confided in me that she was very apprehensive about the marriage because she had never met the groom. The marriage had been arranged for her by her parents. She had only seen a picture of the groom and had never talked to him, even on the telephone. Because I often spent the night at her home, I had many opportunities to pray with her about this forthcoming marriage. I tried to reassure her as best I could by telling her that God is a good God and has good plans for her.

The wedding day arrived and I was privileged to be invited to the three-day ceremony. The first day we did henna painting of the hands. This is a favorite artistic expression in their culture. The second day Shapira and all the women gathered together to celebrate. The men gathered separately to celebrate. Later that day there was a separate signing of the marriage papers by Shapira and the groom, with the Imam (minister) present. On the third day the groom came to take Shapira to his home. She was still fully covered so that he could not see her face. After arriving at the groom's home, it was Shapira's mother, not the groom, who removed her veil. In fact, the groom was not even in the room!

The bride and groom did not sleep together that first night. Shapira's older sister, known as the "milk sister," stayed with her that night to comfort her and inform the younger sister about married life. The other sisters and I left and only the milk sister stayed. That was Shapira's first night in her husband's house.

In that culture the trousseau is of great importance. Shapira brought perhaps as many as sixty suits (outfits) for herself and also suits for her mother-in-law and father-in-law. The bride is also expected to bring gifts of furniture such as a television set or a refrigerator. The bride's parents bear the cost of the entire wedding. Imagine if they have many daughters how much they have to save for those weddings. The groom's expense, on the other hand, is negligible.

Dear Shapira. What will her future be like?. Her parents have given her love, culture, and education. They have lovingly tried during her entire lifetime to prepare her for this event. Naturally, they would like for it to be special. The marriage was all arranged for her. She had no say in the matter. Will her husband be respectful and kind to her? Was she right about her fears and apprehensions? We shall see in part two of this story.

Arranged Marriage: Part Two

Story #2 by Ingrid

In the beginning of her new marriage, Shapira's husband seemed to be a nice guy, and she appeared to be happy. But after awhile he started to complain that he wasn't satisfied with her sexually and he wanted her to watch some pornographic movies with him. This disturbed her very much, and I prayed with her about it. A few months into the marriage, she got pregnant and things went a little better for her. Their baby boy was born on my birthday! That was very special to me.

But not long after the baby was born, her husband became violent. He began beating her and they were arguing all the time. When things got bad, she would go back to her home for a few days. This, of course, got her parents involved. Many times she would ask me for prayer. One day she told me she thought she would be better off dead. Her husband had succeeded in convincing her she was not a good wife.

So that she could receive some counseling from a married woman, I have introduced Shapira to a married missionary friend of mine. My friend has been able to counsel and help her, and Shapira is fairly open to talking about the Lord with her.

At Christmas time the team invited Shapira's whole family to hear the Christmas story. They said to us, "When you pray, God is listening to you. He does not hear our prayers." Shapira knows there is a relationship between the Lord and me. She is not yet ready to take the step of accepting Him, but I believe she is very close. My heart goes out to her, and I keep holding her up in prayer.

Life In The Village

Story by Betty

Betty moved to Central Asia as a young single woman. She served there several years before meeting and marrying her husband. They continued on the field as a married couple for several more years before returning to the United States. God has blessed them with a beautiful little daughter. They are now awaiting their next assignment in the Lord's work. Betty gives us some interesting vignettes of Muslim life.

When I first went to this Central Asian country, another young missionary woman and I lived with a village family in order to study the language and get acquainted with the culture. One day I watched in astonishment as the grandmother of the family slit the throat of a sheep and caught the blood in a cup. She then took that blood to a local charm and fetish shop to be sold for use in folk remedies and healings. Another day I observed the grandmother as she put pieces of paper with writing on them, called amulets, in her tea cup and poured hot water over them. Then she drank that water as a way to get healing for her stomach. But she ended up going to the hospital after all.

Sometimes, however, healings occur as a result of their prayers, as

I observed on a particular day. A young cousin who had a sore throat came into the house and plopped down by me on the sofa. To my complete surprise, and his, the mother of the house came and grabbed the boy by the throat and started praying over him. He was very startled and ran away. Then he began vomiting up a lot of mucus fluid. After that, he calmed down and seemed to be okay, with the sore throat all gone! It all happened so quickly. The boy was undeniably much better, if not healed. That is why they keep practicing folk Islam–it often works for them. And they don't know to pray to Jesus.

Before I left that home, I sat down and tried to explain to the mother why my hope is in Jesus. Christianity is such a foreign concept to them. She did not really understand. But I feel that because my roommate and I lived with the family for a number of months, they certainly knew that we were different. They got to see Christians firsthand in daily living. We were new in the culture and perhaps not as aggressive as we could have been in personal witnessing. But we do know that we acted and reacted according to the nature of His love in us, and through that, we are confident that we were the Message to them.

Tamara: Kidnapped Bride

Story #2 by Betty

One of the peculiar customs in the Central Asian country where I was serving is the acceptance of bride kidnapping by a man who wants her for his wife. That is not to say that the traditional courting does not usually take place. It does. But they treat bride kidnapping lightly. They like to think of it as a romantic game or just a fun thing to do, stirring up some excitement. They neglect to consider the lifelong consequences for the girl, who usually is only in her mid-teens. She may be a total stranger to the man, never having met him before, but she is still considered to be fair game. Of course, all the advantages are on the man's side. The girl gets no opportunity to refuse him. During my time in Central Asia I knew of several such kidnapped brides. This is Tamara's story.

Tamara was a happy and beautiful teenager, just fifteen years old when she became the victim of a kidnap plot. A young man, whom she had never met, saw a picture of her at a relative's home and decided right away that he wanted her for his wife. However, he did not want to court her in the traditional way. Perhaps it was out of fear of rejection. Somehow he managed to persuade the girl's own relatives to help him.

They planned a nice party and invited unsuspecting Tamara. One of the relatives had come to pick her up. There was excitement in the air! By the time they arrived at the party, Tamara had become suspicious of something. When she refused to get out of the car, she was pulled out and pushed into the arms of a total stranger! Her tears and pleadings made no difference. She was taken to the kidnapper's home where she was held overnight. The next day her captor called her family to ask their permission to marry the girl. In the eyes of the parents, their daughter had already been violated, and so to bring her back home would be to bring shame on the family.

It was an ill-fated marriage from the beginning. The husband turned out to be an alcoholic and was very abusive to Tamara. She hated him and ran away three times.

Each time he would find her and bring her back. Eventually she became pregnant and a little girl was born. In that culture sons are much more valued than daughters. Her husband was probably disappointed in the girl child. Perhaps for that reason, when Tamara left him again, he gave up the pursuit, and they were divorced. Bitter with what life had dealt her and without much hope for the future, she went to live with her sister in the big city. There she found work and with the help of her family began a new life.

Several years later, Tamara and her two sisters decided, just out of curiosity, to go to a city-wide Christian meeting. It was a new experience for them. They had never been to any church, only to mosques. The message at the meeting was strong and appealing. When the invitation was given, Tamara felt compelled to go forward.

Her angry sisters tried to hold her back but couldn't. That night Tamara was wonderfully saved and gave her heart to the Lord. Her life was totally changed! Her former bitterness and hopelessness were gone. She had an incredible peace and hope in Jesus. God gave her a great love for the lost–in fact, love for everybody she met. She joined a church and began to have a dynamic ministry.

It was several years after this that I first met Tamara. She was helping to plant a church in one of the smaller towns. Our American team went in to help encourage the believers. There Dave, one of my teammates, met and fell in love with Tamara. Her little daughter was by now about seven years old, and Dave was captivated by her, too. Tamara and Dave were married and became a very happy family. Dave chose to be a long-term missionary in that country. They are still serving in Central Asia. The church they planted has now combined with a larger church and is doing very well.

God in His goodness looked down and took pity on this poor, desperate young woman whose youth had been stolen from her and who had been trapped in a loveless marriage. God rescued her, gave her a husband worthy of her, and gave them both a happy and productive life working in His Kingdom!

Oleta: The "Kellen Bride"

Story #3 by Betty

Pity the poor bride who marries the youngest son in the country in Central Asia where I served. She is known as the kellen or "slave daughter-in-law." In this society it is the responsibility of the youngest son to live with and take care of his parents for their whole lives. When he marries, his bride becomes the slave of the mother-in-law and, indeed, of the whole family. She is definitely at the bottom of the family's social strata. Oleta, a kellen bride, found that role difficult enough, but added to that was the bitter disapproval of her mother-in-law. She tells her own story.

Oleta:

I had been teaching at the university for several years when my biological clock told me it was time to get married. I met Beto through mutual friends. He was educated, handsome, and quite charming. I felt myself being drawn to him, but some of my friends cautioned me saying, "You know he is the youngest son and is tied to his mother." I knew I should consider that, but what young woman in love does not think that there is nothing about her man that she cannot manage? And so I, being confident or just plain foolish, decided to take the risk.

119

Beto had taken me to his home only once–so his mother could look me over. If she had any objections to me, Beto never conveyed them to me in any way. At that meeting I found her to be quite pleasant. So I rationalized that I had nothing to fear. We proceeded with the wedding, after which I moved into his parents' home.

However, as the days wore on his mother became increasingly icy to me and I knew I had not won her favor. I knew I was failing the "mother-in-law test." I did not know what more I could do. I was working at the university, doing most of the cooking, waiting on the whole family and the extended family as well. (It seemed that they all came there to have their daily tea.) I tried hard to please everyone and to be a good and acceptable wife, but nothing seemed to work.

I finally came to the conclusion that it was the very happiness that Beto and I shared that triggered her anger. Jealousy and fear were lying just under the surface. She was an uneducated woman and was of the old tradition that did not approve of women working outside the home. I was not only educated but also an educator. It was a power struggle between the old and new culture, and for me and Beto it had devastating results.

It was evident that I would not get any support from him. He could not bring himself to hear a word of criticism about his mother nor allow himself to show much sympathy to me for fear of being disloyal to her. I was on my own and very much alone.

Things came to a head one day when I came home from work and discovered that all of my belongings had been carelessly thrown out on the front porch. She wanted me out of her house, immediately. Now Beto had to choose between me and his mother. It came as no surprise to me or to anyone else that he chose his mother. He always would be more her possession than mine or, for that matter, any other woman's. She had spoiled him all his life and conditioned him to serve her own purposes.

Friends helped me move my belongings back to my parents' home. There, as our custom demands, I would continue to live with my parents as I had before my marriage. It would be a hard time for me because divorced women are looked down upon in our society. The failure of a marriage rests more heavily upon the woman. Yet I refused to blame myself, because with a mother-in-law like mine, what marriage would ever have a chance for success? Fortunately, I still had a good job. I was not at the mercy of any relative for financial support, and I had no young children as a result of the marriage. For these things I was indeed thankful.

I find very little comfort in my religion. Islam teaches that God is impersonal and only expresses himself in the Qur'an. Some of my Christian friends, to whom I have been teaching my language, have been sharing with me about the love of God. They tell me that God cares about what happens to me and still has good plans for my life. This gives me hope and makes me determined to seek Him in a new way.

Betty:

Being a young bride myself at the time, my heart really went out to Oleta. I felt her pain. My friends and I tried to encourage her and give her hope for the future, real hope in Christ.

Oleta's story happens in different versions all over Central Asia. I know of many such unfortunate women who have become the kellen bride, the slave of the mother-in-law. Some are actually "kidnapped brides," while some marriages are formally arranged by parents. It's part of their socio-economic system for the youngest son to live at home and provide for his parents. Furthermore, it's their custom for his bride to become the mother-in-law's slave. Pity the poor unlucky girl who becomes the kellen bride.

My "Heart-friend"

Story by Cynthia

Cynthia is a young married woman. She shares a story about being new to the field, living in a strange culture, and really needing a friend. She tells how God bridged that cultural gap and gave her a true "heart-friend," Maria.

The culture we moved into was very foreign to me as a young wife. Village people would invite themselves over any time and always want to borrow or get something. This was especially the case since we were "rich" Americans. I found it very hard to adjust to this culture. It made me want to just close my doors to them.

I had been on the field for a while without really connecting with anyone. While we were on home assignment, a very compassionate woman saw my pain. She prayed for me that when I returned to the field I would find a real "heart-friend." And that is exactly what happened!

After furlough, when we returned to the village, my relationship with Maria, a woman I had known but was not close to, suddenly flourished. She became my language helper. And as our friendship deepened, we were able to talk together about things that were important to us. It was a happy friendship in both directions.

Previously I had not been comfortable in the "give-and-take" culture we were living in, but with Maria, I had the feeling that we could not "out-give" each other. That aspect of the culture that can best be expressed as, "If you need something I will give it and if I need something you will give it," happened between us!

When Maria asked me for something, I never had the feeling that she was just trying to get something from me. Maybe she was somewhat cautious about that, not wanting to step over the line of proper conduct. The important thing was that our friendship was comfortable. It was so close and deep that we could talk about whatever I could get my language around. I know it was an answer to prayer, and it helped me at a difficult point in my missionary journey.

I was enjoying our friendship and assumed we were going to have lots more time together. Little did I know our time would be so short. Suddenly one day my husband and I were ordered by the government to leave the country! I had to say goodbye to Maria on the public telephone. She was weeping and so was I.

Until we were expelled from the country, I never knew how badly I wanted to be there, or how much I would miss my dear heart-friend, Maria. I continue to pray for her, knowing all these things are in God's hands.

"Love is the outpouring of one personality in fellowship with another personality." -Oswald Chambers

Umeda Finds Hope

Story by Laura

The following story was told to me by a beautiful 15-year-old whose parents served in Central Asia. As you can tell from her story, she has a heart for evangelism and is a true Daybreaker. This is Laura's story of how she helped one of her school friends find hope.

My name is Laura and this story is about one of my classmates, Umeda. In the beginning, Umeda and I did not know each other very well. We just said "Hello" and "Goodbye." But it wasn't long before we got better acquainted.

One day a few of us girls decided to go bike riding. Since I was the only one with a bike, we had to take turns. We were having fun, and all went well until it was Umeda's turn. Since this was only the second time she had ever tried to ride a bike, she was having some trouble keeping her balance. The other girls grew impatient with her and started getting mad at her and yelling at her. Suddenly Umeda got off the bike and ran away crying. We all followed after her, and the girls who had done the yelling apologized and asked if something else was wrong, but she did not want to talk to any of us. The other girls left, but I felt I needed to stay and talk with her.

When we were alone, she began telling me about her family. She said her father was an alcoholic and that he abused her mother and her and her brothers. She was really angry at her father and wished she could have a better life. She told me that she would go to school just to be happy a few hours. Then she said that for the past week she had just wanted to die because she had nothing to live for.

How sad I felt that Umeda, whose name means "hope," was so hopeless. I saw her as someone who needed Jesus, and I began to share with her about how much Jesus loved her. I asked her if she would like to know Him and repent of her sins. She accepted Jesus and it was very exciting! I realized as I shared with Umeda that God was helping me because at that time I didn't know her language very well. He was helping me share with her and say the right things about Him and the Bible. It was very powerful!

The next morning I met Umeda on the way to school. She came up to me with a big smile on her face and said, "Guess what, Laura? I woke up this morning and for the first time in my entire life I felt truly happy!" She continued to express how God had blessed her.

Today she is a passionate believer. She has been bringing girls in my neighborhood to a Bible study. She does have her ups and downs. But it's such a blessing to see that Umeda now has hope, real hope in Jesus.

"Except ye be converted and become as little children..." (Matt.18:3 KJV)

Esmat Chooses Her Husband

Story by Jennifer

Jennifer and her husband have lived in the Middle East for two and a half years. They have an adorable little daughter, 14 months old, born in the country where they serve. Jennifer tells an interesting story of how her friend, Esmat, navigated some dangerous waters before marriage to negotiate with her prospective father-in-law for her husband, Joel, the man she loved.

One day I decided to venture out in my neighborhood for a stroll to the market. We live in an apartment building up on the third floor, which makes it difficult to get out with my little daughter. Also my country has a dress code to observe–the wearing of a chador. A chador is a robe that goes over a woman's street clothing and can be very warm and uncomfortable on a nice spring day. Nevertheless, I was glad I made the effort to get out that day because I met my neighbor and now my good friend, Esmat.

While I was in the market, a woman who was also wearing a chador and with a child about five years old came up to me, introduced herself and asked me if I lived around there. It turned out she lived just two doors down from me in the same apartment building. Esmat was the first woman from my apartment building whom I had met, even though I had lived there for several months. She was so friendly and, of course, was interested in my little daughter. Esmat invited me to come over and have tea with her. Although my language was not very good, she was patient with me and we had a nice visit. I enjoyed her wonderful sense of humor and we had a lot of fun together.

One day Esmat told me a funny story. She said that when she was young, she had two suitors, both courting her at the same time. One of them was her cousin, whom she did not want to marry. The other was Joel, a young seminary student of Islamic law, to whom she was very attracted. According to the custom of their country, the whole family of a suitor will just "drop in" for a visit at the home of the intended. One night both suitor families dropped in on the same night! It was very awkward for Esmat and her family because it was like having two dates at the same time. Somehow she and her family managed to get through that embarrassing evening, and they can laugh about it now.

Esmat's parents were more favorable to her marrying her cousin, who was financially stable. But she made up her mind and made it known that she had no intention of marrying her cousin. Her heart belonged only to Joel.

Her father's objection to this match was his fear that Joel could not sufficiently provide for his daughter. After all, he was just a young seminary student, working part-time with no means to support a wife. Undeterred, Esmat showed herself to be very clever and resourceful in her plans to marry the man she really loved.

She realized that she needed a way to reassure her father that Joel could support her. She said to him, "If I negotiate with Joel's father so that he will give me some plots of land and other property as a sort of deposit or down payment, guaranteeing that his son will provide for me when he finishes seminary, will that satisfy you?" Her father said, "Yes. If you can do that, it will put my heart at ease that you will be provided for."

Then Esmat bravely approached her prospective father-in-law about the whole proposition–and he agreed! No doubt he admired Esmat for her resourcefulness and spirit of determination and thought she would make a good wife for his son.

So the marriage took place, and it turned out to be a very good one. Her husband is very respectful of her and gives her freedom. She does not work outside the home even though she is college educated. He makes a good living for the family and is studying for his doctorate in Islamic law. They have a 14-year-old son and two daughters, nine and five years old.

Esmat has been a very good friend and neighbor. She has helped me learn to cook ethnic dishes. In this society there are no cookbooks! Girls learn to cook from their mothers and from aunts and grandmothers. Everything is just passed down from one generation to the next, and they learn by doing.

A number of times Esmat has rescued me from mealtime disaster when I was expecting guests and my rice was just not turning out right. (This, I might add, was not a simple rice recipe but a four-

or five-step version.) I would call her, and she would throw on her chador, rush over to help me in the kitchen, and when finished, put her chador on again and move through my guests, graciously greeting them on her way out, never revealing that she had been helping me in the kitchen.

We are able to talk about spiritual things now that my language skills have gotten better. My prayer is that Esmat's understanding of who Isa (Jesus) is will be enlightened and that I will be a blessing to her. Most of the time, I feel that Esmat has given more to me than I have given to her. It is then that I need to review and restate to myself what is the purpose of my life. Did I not leave country and family and friends and travel half way around the world just to meet someone like Esmat? And did not Christ say that out of me should "flow rivers of living water" so that others would be refreshed? I know that I am a witness for Jesus, that I am His, and that He is carrying out His purposes through me, even when I am not aware of it.

Kendra Marries A Christian

Story by Jeanine

Jeanine and her husband have been on the field in Asia for 14 years. She tells of her friendship with two young Muslim women. One story ends in joy and the other in sadness. Each story will give you some insight into the culture of Islam.

Kendra, a very beautiful and intelligent young Muslim woman, worked in the office at the Blind Center where I taught English as a second language. She got acquainted with several young blind men there. And one, Ben, was a Christian. As Kendra got better acquainted with Ben, she also wanted to know more about Christianity. So we gave her some helpful books to read and explained Scriptural truth to her . She accepted the Lord and was excited about her new faith. She quickly wanted to move ahead and be baptized. We were cautious because in her culture this is a huge step. Being convinced of her sincerity, my husband agreed to baptize her and Ben also, who had never been baptized although he came from a Christian background.

We were very concerned when we learned that Kendra and Ben had fallen in love and wanted to get married. In the country where we serve, for a Muslim woman to marry a Christian poses a huge problem. And for that reason, Muslims and Christians rarely marry. Islam is not just a religion; it is a whole culture. If you are Muslim, you are regarded as a part of that culture. And if you leave, you are treated badly, even by your own family. There have even been many instances where young girls have been killed by their own fathers for becoming Christians. So this was a very serious move, not only for Kendra but for Ben too. His life and the lives of his family could be threatened. However, they persisted in their determination to marry.

My husband and I had them in our home often. We counseled them and prayed with them. We had them talk first to Ben's parents, who, even though they were very scared, gave their consent to the marriage.

Kendra decided she would not inform her family of her plans until after the marriage. However, she and Ben did not live together after the marriage until Kendra went back to her family and said, "You didn't come to the wedding, but I am now married and you need to give me away as is the custom." And so they did! They gave a great party for the couple in their home, inviting family and friends. Because they loved their daughter, they no doubt wanted to be a part of her life and do the right thing. They have accepted Kendra back into the family and have accepted Ben as her husband. Now the family sees their happiness and how good the marriage is.

It's been a few years since their marriage, and they now have a beautiful son about two years old. In many ways Kendra has chosen a difficult path, with Ben being blind and with her departure from Islam. But they are a very courageous couple. My husband and I continue to counsel and encourage them, and we continue to pray for their safety. Even at this point in their lives there is still a lot of danger for them. But they are very happy together, and it is a joy to see them grow in their faith. This has been very rewarding to us.

Sita: Runaway Teen

Story #2 by Jeanine

While teaching English to young girls, I have had the opportunity to minister to many of them, often counseling those who wanted to run away from home and helping by being there and listening to them. Sita was one such girl. We loved her and had a great interest in her. She had already become a believer and was baptized. She was very intelligent, eager to learn, and wanted desperately to go on to college. However, she had one problem. This is her story.

One day Sita came into my class very upset. When I questioned her about what was bothering her, she said it was because her step-mother would not let her go to college and had been treating her badly, and that very day had threatened to have Sita's brothers beat her up. She said she was fearful and did not want to go home anymore and wanted to stay with us. Now you don't take a Muslim girl into your home lightly, because her family can call the police and cause a lot of trouble. In spite of our misgivings and because we loved Sita, we said to her, "Okay, you can come in and we will help you to think it all out."

Later that night her father came looking for her. He was really very angry and upset. From him we learned that the woman Sita had called her step-mother was actually her real mother. She was a very traditional Muslim woman who did not want her daughter to be exposed to the outside world, nor did she want her to be educated. It was against her that Sita had rebelled. She refused to go home with her father even after talking for two hours. So we said to the father, "Why don't you let her stay for a few days and she will come back home. You will see. It will be all right."

The father said to us, "Before I came into your home I was very angry and very upset, but as soon as I walked into your house, even though I had never met you before, there was a peace which covered me that I have never experienced before. You know, as a Muslim, I won't leave my daughter even in my own brother's house, but with God and you folks, I can leave my daughter here." So he left Sita with us.

We talked to Sita more about salvation, and she said she believed in Christ and that she knew He was her Savior. We knew she had been baptized. After three days I suggested I would buy her some new clothes because she came to us with just the clothes she was wearing. But she said, "Oh, no, I have clothes at home. I will just go home and get them and I will be back." That was her intent.

When she went home she called us and said, "My father has not eaten nor drunk anything for the three days I have been gone. I can't bear to see him die like this. So is it okay if I just stay home?" Although we were fearful of the outcome, we said to her, "Sita, remember that whatever comes your way, Christ can help and the God of Scripture is real."

Sita called once more to say that everything was going to be fine, that she was going to be allowed to continue her education and things were much better. However, her family deceived her. Within two weeks of her return, Sita was married off to a relative. Of course, once married, she was under the complete control and domination of her husband.

We never heard from dear Sita again. We hope the husband was someone compatible to her in age and one who would be kind to her. We can only plant the seeds and trust they will bear fruit. We can invest in lives, but we have to leave the outcome with God.

Faithful Narnie

Story by Suzanne

Suzanne is a very remarkable woman. People are attracted to her friendly, open personality and deep spiritual qualities. She and her husband have lived for 15 years in Central Asia. They have three great kids. They recently felt God's call to a new and different country, which means learning a new language and many other changes. Suzanne has a great heart and knows how to evangelize. She brings spiritual depth to her discipling, as you will see in her story about Narnie.

Narnie has become a dear sister in the Lord. Her husband is not a believer and often is in a foul mood. Two nights ago Narnie left our house and headed home. Our Bible study that day had been on being still and waiting on God, learning to listen to His voice in every situation. While on the bus ride home she read the following verse.

2 Corinthians 4:16-18 *"Therefore we do not lose heart. Though outwardly we are wasting away, yet inwardly we are being renewed day by day. For our light and momentary troubles are achieving for us an eternal glory that far outweighs them all. So we fix our eyes not on what is seen, but what is unseen. For what is seen is temporary,*

but what is unseen is eternal." As she read she pondered what it really meant. She was soon to find out.

Upon arriving home, she found that her husband, Bart, was in a very bad mood. She pressed him and asked what was troubling him. He replied, "Even though I gave you permission to read the Bible, I didn't mean it. You are a Muslim and you must only read the Qur'an. You must act like a Muslim woman. I forbid you to do anything differently again." At that moment she sensed God's hand telling her to speak kindly, but she didn't listen. Responding in anger, she yelled back. The argument escalated and he snapped, brutally beating her.

When she arrived at our home two days later, she had one black eye, bruises up and down both arms and legs, and a deep cut on one cheek. With anger rising in me and tears streaming down my cheeks, I asked her what happened. I already knew Bart had done it. To my surprise, Narnie replied with a beaming smile, "Be still, my sister, and listen to the joy of my Lord."

She said that after Bart had beaten her for over thirty minutes, she stopped him dead in his tracks by saying, "You can beat me all you want; you can take my life away, But I will not stop being a follower of Jesus who is Lord and King! I will not stop reading the Holy Word of God!"

At that Bart tore up the Bible and threw it at her, and said, "Where did you get this? Did Suzanne give this to you again? She is trying to change you from our traditions."

Narnie replied, "Bart, you have sinned against Holy God by

tearing up His Word. You will have to repent of your ways. You have asked me to be like other Muslim women, but can you not see the difference in me since Jesus came into my life and transformed me? He has made me new! He has caused me to have a deeper love for you and for our son. He has shown me how to give you the respect you deserve, how to truly love. Have you not seen the difference in me? And now you ask that I return to what I was? That is impossible and just stupidity."

Bart nodded his head and said, "Yes, that is true. I have seen a great change in you."

"My dear man," said Narnie, "that is Jesus, and only He, which you are seeing. I can no longer live without Him in my life. That would be like taking the very breath I breathe out of my lungs. If you have to divorce me and take another woman like the ones who will be Muslim for you, then you must. This same Jesus who died on the cross for the whole world's sin wants this transforming love for you. I hope this for you, and for our son, but I will not deny Jesus and the Holy Spirit who lives in me, for you or anyone! So again, I say divorce me if you must, and take on the women who gossip and say they are God-fearing. Take one who will read the Qur'an and then do the opposite of serving God. It is for you to decide."

With tears streaming down his face, Bart fell on his knees, begging her forgiveness. "No, Narnie, I don't want any other woman, I only want you. Most men in our culture have a wife or two, and a mistress, but I only want you. I don't want a divorce. Read what you want, believe what you want. I will not divorce you!"

No wonder Narnie was beaming with joy! She has asked my husband and me and another believing couple to come to her house Saturday night for a meal. We are going to share the Gospel with Bart and talk to him about signing a new marriage covenant with Narnie.

Oh, the wondrous love of God and its ability to transform giants into mice and mice into giants.

Tale Of Three Ladies

Story #2 by Suzanne

This is the tale of three ladies, Narnie, Free and Dell. Narnie is thriving in her walk with our Lord, although she has had some deep valleys. She has endured beatings from her husband, leaving and returning to her home, illness of her son, fear of her family finding out she has left their ways, and countless little troubles. Yet through it all she has chosen Jesus and keeps pressing on. I have been studying the Word of God with her since she accepted Christ as her Savior in October, and to her credit, she has stuck with the studying. That is a miracle in itself, as my language skills are still so new that it is an uphill battle to convey the beauty of the Gospel with my feeble words.

God answered our prayers by bringing another believer to our door. We call her Free. Free has been a believer for six years now. She and I have had several talks. She is a very educated woman, speaks some English, and is a trained nurse. She has consented to join with me in the training-up of Narnie. She said today that this is the first time in six years that she ever had the courage to share with another, and teaching the Word is making her grow all the more. What a joy to see these ladies sharing, laughing, crying, and touching each other's hearts. Free fills in the gaps in my language and quickly helps direct the conversation to the point.

Narnie invited her sister-in-law to come and meet with us weekly as well. We will call her Dell. So now we have three. Praise God! These three are remarkable together. One asks a question and another starts to answer, then they look at me and say, "Is that right?" I say, "Let's look at the Word for the answer." We then turn to the passage and I say, "Now, how would you answer that question?" After this happened three times in a row, one of the ladies said, "Let's look at the Word; we shouldn't ask Suzanne as she is fallible." Then she slapped me on the leg and laughed. I said, "That's so true. And God gave His Spirit of wisdom to you to find the answer in His unchanging Word!" This is so much fun! What a good and precious God we serve!

So rejoice with me as we four study together and learn from His Word all that He has for us and for our families. Pray for all three of these ladies, Narnie, Dell, and Free as they all have unbelieving husbands who also need to come to know Jesus as Lord and Savior.

Parvina Finds Jesus

Story by Elizabeth

The following story is by a beautiful teen-age girl who has spent a good part of her life in a country in Central Asia. She has a great heart for evangelism, born out of compassion for her young Muslim friends and her love for the Lord.

My name is Elizabeth. I live with my parents in Central Asia, and for the past three years I have been attending a local school there. That is where I met Parvina, a classmate of mine who became my good friend. As we became acquainted, she began opening up and sharing with me her fears and some problems in her life. I found out that her father abuses her and once even stabbed her in the leg. She was a girl living in fear, and she felt worthless and insignificant in her family and even at school.

Through learning that, I was able to minister to her and share the love of Jesus with her. I gave her a Bible in her own language, which she began reading. Then she decided to give her life to Jesus and become a Christian, even though she knew it would mean opposition from her parents and Muslim friends. As she found the love of Jesus, she began sharing with such great faith. And she would not pray a usual prayer that most people would pray, for example, to bless the food or the household, but she would pray from her heart as though she knew Jesus as her best friend. It has been amazing seeing her boldness and strong Christian witness.

One day she was having a sleep-over with one of her friends at her grandmother's house. They were talking when suddenly they saw something moving around in the yard. They both thought it was some kind of evil spirit. You see, for her people, the fear of demons is very real and they are constantly afraid that the "evil eye" is going to harm them in some way. So Parvina's friend began praying a prayer to Allah to protect her. Parvina remembered the Scripture that at the name of Jesus demons had to flee and that Satan had no power over Jesus. Parvina began speaking the name of Jesus and began telling her friend about the miracles Jesus had performed on this earth and about his life. Her friend suddenly stopped and realized that all her fear was gone! She said, "When I was praying in the name of Allah my fear was still in my heart, but when you said the name of Jesus, my fear was gone. I want to know more about Jesus."

Parvina continues to grow in the Lord and share Him with others. It is wonderful to see her go from being so fearful to having such boldness and joy in the Lord.

Iman: Professional Musician

Story by Claire

Claire, a single woman, has worked in Central Asia for nine years. She is one of our many Frontiers ladies who have answered the call of God to be used in His redemptive work in the world.

Several years ago I was interested in learning the national musical instrument of this culture and realized I needed a good teacher. A co-worker of mine recommended Iman, who has received one of her nation's highest honors for musical achievement and has been honored by the president of her country. In contrast to many of the women I work with who come from village backgrounds, Iman was very well educated. Although she did not earn a lot of money, she was higher up in the social stratum and because of that she was very confident.

In this country it is very important to show your qualifications. If one has received awards or honorariums or been recognized for doing something special, these accolades are all displayed. So, on my very first visit Iman showed me all her awards and where she got her degree. I really wasn't much interested in all that. I was just interested in learning that musical instrument. But, because I could see these things were very important to her, I listened politely.

The instrument I wanted to play, which resembles a banjo, turned out to be quite difficult to learn, but God gave me the grace to stick with it. Over time, Iman could see that I was not going to be one of her top students who majors in music at the local institute and who practices hours every day. After all, I had a job and I just didn't have the time to practice that much. Eventually, she and I reached an agreement on what I could actually deliver and what her expectations should be. I was delighted when she taught me to play some worship songs she had learned from previous students who were also believers. There was one, her favorite, which she wanted us to play at every session.

I learned that Iman had taught many missionary workers to play this instrument and that they had all shared the Gospel with her in varying ways. On different occasions I would share with her stories of the Old Testament to which she would listen politely, but then she would frequently go off on a tangent. She was interested in reading spiritual books, not just the Qur'an and the Bible, but other books in which she learned what she thought were good spiritual things.

One day when I came for a lesson, Iman sent me into the room where we had our lesson and then went out again. When she came back into the room, I could see she had been crying. I asked her what was wrong. At first she didn't want to talk about it, but she finally told me that her mother had just been diagnosed with breast cancer. Even worse was that although her mother had been complaining about symptoms for a long time, she had refused to go in for a diagnosis, acting against the urging of Iman and her sister. By the time her mother did go in for an exam, doctors said it was too late to do much for her. So Iman was hearing that her mother was going to die. Of course, she was very sad to hear that.

I asked if I could pray for her and her mother in Jesus' name. She agreed to that, and so I prayed for her. At that point our relationship began to change. She began to think of me more as a friend, not just one of her students. She had always been very kind to me, even introducing me to her parents when they came to visit her. I knew her twin sister because the two of them lived together. I had also met the younger sister as well. I just felt really comfortable with them. Sometimes when I came for a lesson and hadn't yet had lunch, she would make lunch for me. So our relationship developed to a new level.

The next year passed, and her mother, instead of dying as the doctors had expected, kept getting stronger. But then another tragedy struck unexpectedly. Her father was diagnosed with cancer and lived just a month or so before he passed away. Because the doctor bills mounted up so high, Iman and her sister leased out their apartment in the city and moved back home to be with their mother, commuting to work from the village to the city each day.

I deemed it a great honor to be invited to their father's funeral in the village. It was a cultural experience to be there. There was much crying and wailing. There must have been over 300 people gathered there. I was the only foreigner. Iman looked very different, with no make-up and her head covered, very unlike the chic young urban woman that I was used to seeing.

Not long after that I heard that *The Passion of the Christ* video was available in local stores. Because I knew that Iman could not afford it, I bought it for her. Although she had no VCR, her neighbors did and they all got together to watch it. So it was even better that they all got to see it instead of just Iman. That next week my lesson was delayed quite a bit as she had to tell me the whole story and also had some questions to ask. She was so animated and excited about it. That was awesome to me.

A couple of weeks later she stayed up very late, until 2:00 a.m., to watch the entire Jesus film on television. She was so touched by the scene on the cross and found it very troubling to her. She said, "Yes, that whole scene where He was on the cross, it was so troubling to me, especially after watching [*The Passion*]. When they led in that prayer afterwards, I prayed that too." I knew that she was running late and was on her way out the door, but I quickly asked, "Really, but why did you pray?" She said, "I prayed it because I didn't want to have bad dreams that night." To which I replied, "Well, did you have bad dreams?" "No, I didn't," she said. So I let her go and couldn't press her further.

God knows where she is with all this. He used simple things, like worship songs, Bible stories, the videos, and the very constancy of getting together with her every week to teach me a musical instrument, to plant seeds in her heart. And we actually became very good friends over the course of those three years.

When it was time for me to take leave, I invited Iman to my going-away party. She got a chance to see a whole group of believers interact with each other. Even though I wasn't sure about her salvation, I felt that she was now closer to the Kingdom than she was when I first met her. I am trusting God to take those seeds planted and do something wonderful with them.

Dangerous Venture

Story by Jane

Jane, her husband, and their three children are a courageous and venturous family. They served in a remote, mountainous, Middle Eastern country for five years. Jane tells of some of the real dangers they faced almost constantly while living there. At one point of discouragement, Jane questioned God as to what her own role in missions was. She shares some insights that God revealed to her, insights which can be useful to us all. Through those dark days, Jane learned to abide in Him. God engineered her circumstances there to make her into the strong, independent woman of faith she is today.

D anger became a part of our daily lives in the country where we lived. Neighbors would come and tell us that they had been approached to place a bomb in our house! When we would ask them, "Do you want us to leave?" they would all answer a resounding, "No! We do not want you to leave. It is our honor to protect you."

I remember God kept me strong through one very terrifying ordeal. My husband, Ben, had been given the opportunity to go to another town, about eight hours away by car, with a local believer to teach. They would be away most of six weeks. There were no telephones or cell phones, just those little short-wave radios from the U.N. Communication came through to me that some trouble makers in that town were threatening Ben's life and the lives of the several men who had accompanied him. Ben and the others took the threat seriously. I was so afraid. Our closest team members lived about an hour away from me. One of the wives drove all the way up to our town to sit with me all that day and pray. It was really a hard time for me.

Meanwhile, in the town where Ben was, he and his friends met with the townspeople and put the question squarely before them: Did they want the visitors to stay and teach or to leave? The people voted to have them stay. So Ben and his friends decided to call the bluff of those threatening voices and stayed. As a result of that meeting, ten men came to the Lord!

About two months after that wonderful meeting we heard that an outside faction came into that town and completely demolished the language-learning center where my husband had done his teaching. Again, we were thankful for God's protection over him and his team.

In spite of the opposition, the work continued to go forward. Later that summer our family drove down to that town when the ten were baptized as a result of that meeting. It all took place outside of town by a river and was a time of real rejoicing and singing. We heard many give testimony of their faith in Jesus.

After I had been in the country for awhile, I seemed to lose some of my zeal for being there. I had come to believe that my role was just so invisible. I asked myself, "What am I doing here?" Then, in my regular Bible reading, God brought before me the teaching in I Corinthians 12 about the body of Christ having many parts and how they all work together for the glory of God. He showed me that although my part was not visible, yet I did have an important role in His call to that land–and after that I was quite contented to be there.

I have fond memories of my good friend and neighbor, Dove, the baker lady. She was the wife of a leader in our neighborhood, and we tried to cultivate their friendship. My son and hers would often play together. She was a high energy person and had a little bakery business going on in her home. Her house had the typical flat roof of that country, and Dove had built a clay oven there where she baked bread and other goodies and sold them in the neighborhood. The bread was not in loaves as we know it but rather like a large tortilla. I can still smell the delicious aroma of her fresh baked bread as it wafted out over the neighborhood from her rooftop bakery.

Somehow Dove got wind of my "famous" chocolate cake and often would commission me to bake one for her family. I was glad to oblige but would ask her to furnish the butter, eggs, and sugar.

My frequent prayer was, "Oh, Lord, give me opportunity to speak into Dove's life." I trust that He did that through my actions, my parenting, and how I lived in the neighborhood. She was very open to conversations about God–God answering prayer, healing, and the sovereignty of God. Sometimes I would talk to Dove about the sacrifice of Jesus and how she did not have to prove herself through good works to be accepted by God, but rather that Jesus was our sacrifice. She never came to faith while I was there, but God helped me share my faith with her. Good seeds were sown and I know they made an impact.

We shared some hard times together. I prayed with her often when one of her daughters made an unfortunate marriage and had to come back home. To their credit, Dove and her husband were very loving and received her back into their home. Some young girls in this society are not so lucky. When their marriages fail, they become so desperate and hopeless that they actually douse themselves with gasoline and set themselves on fire. So very terrible!

As I look back on those years of ministry in that hard place, I think of them as an adventure with God. I know they served His purpose in my life in so many ways.

God gave us fruit in our ministry. We met many good and loving people and introduced them to the love of Jesus. And all the while God, in His own amazing way, was maturing us for our next adventure with Him.

"…kept by the power of God…" (I Peter 1:5 KJV)

"How Many Women Does It Take To Clean A Turkish Carpet?"

Story by Gloria

Gloria has served for a number of years in Central Asia. This amusing story shows her love for her neighbors and how the most menial of tasks–carpet cleaning–can become a fun-filled group activity. Enjoy!

How many women does it take? Usually, just one. But if the carpet owner happens to be a foreigner–well, let me tell you. As you may know, Turks take their shoes off before entering a home. That is why I am not ashamed to tell you that in six years I have cleaned my carpets only once. Don't misunderstand. I regularly vacuum them and shake them out ritually before all the Turkish religious holidays like any gossip-fearing Turkish woman. But in six years I have actually washed them once and that was by sending them out to the professional cleaners while we were out of town. In the big cities that is what most Turkish women do. But that is not so in our little town. Here, real women wash their own carpets. This is important because in Turkey, when it comes to cleaning, there is the way "every Turkish woman does things," and then there is "the wrong way." I had been avoiding this carpet-cleaning thing because most likely I was destined to do it the wrong way.

Yesterday, however, I saw my landlady and her sister out on the sidewalk scrubbing away at the carpet. What chance! I peeked out from my second floor window and got the basic idea down. Aha! So that's it, is it? I can do that.

I went out with all the needed supplies—bucket, hose, scrub brush (long and short handled) and Arabic soap. Here you don't even think of cleaning without your Arabic soap. It is the number one supply, and let me tell you, you feel like an expert when you have it in hand. Last, I brought out the four-meter hall carpet. (For those of you who failed the metric system in math class, that's about twelve feet.) I got right down to business hosing off the carpet and started scrubbing away. Within seconds I was puffing and looking down the length of this carpet thinking, "This will take hours!" Then out of her gate strolls sweet Nilufer. "Hmm," she says, "I'll be back with my scrub brush." Back she comes with her scrub brush and four neighborhood children, one of them being mine. So we start scrubbing away.

"What soap are you using?" she asks.

"Arabic soap," I proudly reply.

"Hmmm," she says again in that way of hers, "I always use detergent."

Now it's my turn. "Hmmm."

As we approach the end of the carpet, another woman walks by and says, "Kolay Gelsin! (May it come easy to you!) What soap are you using? You sure don't have many bubbles there."

"Arabic soap," we say.

"Oh no, that will make colors dark! I always use detergent. It bubbles up real nice." She walks off again saying, "Kolay gelsin".

Nilufer and I laugh. "Well," I remark, "my landlady said Arabic soap was the best, but this is the first time I have ever done this, so I'll get some detergent and we can run over it again real quick. After all, I think it needs it twice." My arms and knees are already tired from the first twelve-foot run, but down we go to wash again from start to finish, this time with detergent. We are just nearing the end of the second twelve-foot run when Nursen rides up on her bike. Nursen is the cleanest housekeeper on our street, if not in all of Turkey.

"Kolay gelsin!" she says cheerfully. "What soap are you using?"

"Well, we first tried Arabic soap and we are now using detergent," I say, thinking one of those will satisfy her.

"Oh no! You have to use Pril! It will get it sparkling clean!"

"You mean the dish soap?" I ask, a little incredulous.

"Yes, the dish soap! You know it cuts grease and gets out stains. I use it on all my carpets."

"Well, we've gone over this twice. Next time I do carpets I'll be sure to come call you."

"Wait a minute," she says, getting off her bike. "Let me put my stuff away and I'll be right out."

I look over at skinny little Nilufer, who just grins and shrugs her shoulders. I stoop to pick up the hose and when I stand I see green lines up and down the carpet. I blink, thinking I must have stood up too fast and the blood rushing to my head has caused my eyes to see green. But no, it's Nursen pouring Pril all over my carpet! She grabs her long-handled super scrub brush and starts attacking my carpet as if it has cholera.

"Oh, wow! Look at all this dirt! Wow, is this ever dirty!" she repeats several times as she works her way up and down the rug. Within minutes she has scrubbed, flipped, rinsed, and wrung that baby out and has it rolled up dripping water. Nilufer and I stand there staring at it.

Esengul calls down from her balcony, "Kolay gelsin! I'd come help, but my arm is in a cast. Should I put tea on? Can't you come up for tea?"

One by one we decline. It's already 4:30 and that means time to start getting dinner on as the husbands will soon start coming home. I heartily thank Nursen for her expertise and help as she hustles off with brush and Pril in hand.

Then I stand to talk a bit more with Nilufer. She is very poor.

They cannot make ends meet on her husband's salary from the tea shop where he recently found work. They are slowly working their way out of debt, but even so have to move from their home across from me to the depot of the apartment building next to ours in order to save even more on rent. Her debts are not from overspending, but from being unable to pay electric, water, and grocery bills in the past year. I ask Nilufer if the new place is clean enough. She says that it needs paint and the floor is bare cement, but she thinks it will be better than the moldy place she is in now.

Turkish people! So often they frustrate me to death! But today I realize again why I love them so much. The most menial task becomes a group activity, and they can even make carpet cleaning fun. They know what to do and they probably felt great showing this foreigner how to clean a carpet. They would never have stood by and watched while I tried to attack that thing on my own. Come to think of it, I can't recall a time when we had to work or figure things out without help.

How many Turkish women does it take to clean a carpet? It takes only one, but you will never see her doing it alone.

The Journey's End

Story by Edna Lewis

Edna Lewis is a woman to be celebrated! In December 2005 she and her husband, Charles, retired after ministering 36 years in Indonesia. In her work as a nurse, Edna faced many set-backs and disappointments, mostly due to bureaucratic prejudice. Yet, as you will see in my interview with her, she contributed greatly to the health and well-being of every community she served. Charles says Edna deserves a Mother Teresa Award, if such an award were given. Here is a brief interview recounting her remarkable story.

Interviewer: Edna, we know that you went to the field as a married lady. Can you give us some background as to who felt the call first, you or Charles?

Edna: That's an interesting part of our story. Actually, we both had received our call to the mission field long before we ever met. It's safe to say I received my call first, since I was only four years old!

When my aunt came home on furlough from China where she was a missionary nurse, she showed us many fascinating pictures of little forlorn Chinese children. My heart went out to them and I decided, at age four, that when I grew up I would become a nurse like my aunt and go to China to help those little children.

When I was ten years old, a young man from a Bible college in Portland came to our logging camp and held a Daily Vacation Bible School. It was through that man's witness that my parents received Christ that summer. At that time I also gave my heart to the Lord and dedicated my life to Him. From then on my main goal was becoming a missionary nurse. Yet I had no specific calling to a particular people and was willing to go anywhere the Lord directed.

Charles was born to missionary parents in China and raised there. Long before we met he knew he was going to the mission field. His call to the Muslim world came while he was a student in college working with international students. He even took a correspondence course from Pakistan!

Interviewer: Everyone loves a love story–so tell us how you and Charles met.

Edna: He and I met while in university (different schools) at an InterVarsity leadership training camp. He had been elected the new president of his chapter on campus. He came with a bad back injury that happened just the day before he was to leave for the conference. Because I was in leadership, I had also gone to the training camp. I was acting as camp nurse and therefore designated to do the hot pack treatment on Charles' back. However, sparks did not fly at that meeting. Our relationship during the conference was all quite platonic. The lights didn't come on until later when Charles was telling his friend Jerry, who had just gotten married during the summer, that he had met a cute gal at the camp who was one of the bridesmaids in Jerry's wedding. Jerry replied, "Oh, you mean Edna, that girl who is going to be a missionary?" Well, that got Charles' attention! He got busy to find out how he could contact me eighty miles away with no car. You might say that our romance started from there.

Interviewer: Tell us something about those early years.

Edna: Before marriage I earned a BS in nursing education. I also worked in intensive care at a university hospital. After marriage I taught while my husband completed his theological education. Charles entered Fuller Seminary to earn his Master of Divinity, and I got a great job in Los Angeles and got my PHT (Putting Hubby Through!).

My first cross-cultural assignment allowed me to work in Public Health while serving under the U.S. Bureau of Indian Affairs with the Navajo Nation.

Our family's first overseas assignment was in Indonesia. By that time we had two American-born sons, and eventually I gave birth to a daughter and another son in Indonesia.

Interviewer: Did you face any hazards to the family's health during those early years of ministry?

Edna: Health-wise, we had some frightening times, but God was always faithful. Our oldest son almost died of cholera, but I was able to contact medical help by phone and kept him covered with ice and a fan blowing on him to keep his fever from going past 105 degrees. Our daughter had a slight case of polio, with high fever and convulsions. We borrowed a car and rushed her to the hospital in time for the doctor to treat her fever, bringing it down to a safer level.

While in a vacation beach area, and seven months pregnant with baby Cal, I had a severe fall which brought on contractions. I was carried by rickshaw to a local public health clinic that just happened to have a doctor present. I took his advice to go back to the hotel and rest in bed for two to three days. No medical evacuation was needed. Cal's arrival did come a bit early because another rickshaw ride in our city speeded up the delivery!

When a gastro-intestinal attack hit our eight-year-old son, we sensed a demonic attack, but with a local doctor diagnosing appendicitis, we agreed to take him three hours away to the Baptist hospital. On arrival his pains were gone! After a night in the hospital for observation he was released with no symptoms.

Many other missionary wives discovered my diagnostic skills and appreciated my medical attention in a number of crises, like whooping cough and other childhood diseases.

Interviewer: Did you home-school your children in those early years?

Edna: Yes, part of the time we home-schooled and part of the time the children went to a boarding school. When we did home-school, we helped lead a home-school for our own children and other children as well, twelve in all, ranging in age from six to thirteen.

Interviewer: Tell us about your missionary career as a nurse.

Edna: During our second term, we lived in a provincial capital city, but ministered in a primitive region just two hours out of town. I worked with an Indonesian nurse, Esther. She was the wife of a pastor and lived in the city. We two couples operated a village clinic, where there developed a thriving congregation planted by a city church. I remember fondly those days out in the country, developing a strong friendship with Pastor Joseph and Esther.

We later moved up into the mountains to a large Bible college campus. I worked in the campus clinic along with an Indonesian nurse. There I had many experiences with clinically-diagnosed maladies, psychological crises, and also demon possession.

During our fourth term, we moved to a frontier-type community on the west coast of Sumatra. I became more involved with local women's activities. I started an aerobics class for church ladies and Muslim wives of church members. I taught health and led Bible studies. Several Muslim women came to faith. I was much involved with medical care for Bible school students, dealing with TB and many skin and intestinal diseases contracted either on campus or during their village ministries.

Later we were asked to reside at the Southern Sumatra Bible College. There I was campus nurse and counselor dealing with many hygiene and health issues. Teaching health and hygiene to faculty as well as students was a serious need.

By our fifth term, after more than twelve years on the field, we became a part of Frontiers and moved to West Sumatra, a more metropolitan situation, with hospitals and universities with medical schools. I was invited to participate in a Muslim foundation giving aid to poor families for free surgery on hare-lip and cleft palate cases. This led to a request by the foreign donors to have me give an evaluation of the quality of surgeries. I presented the situation honestly, having observed many operations (the sad conditions need not be described here) and within two weeks, I was told my services were no longer needed.

Another time I was invited by the head of the Government Nursing Academy to teach medical English to the senior students. There may have been some suspicion of my religious loyalties, so my time there was only six months!

The same sort of discrimination happened when I was giving exercise classes in a prominent maternity hospital. I had been given permission by the administration to pray in the name of Isa Al Masih for safe gestation and successful delivery. After three years there my time came to an end when one pregnant lady came forth to publicly thank me for our prayers. That was the last straw for the administration, and a polite reason was given to tell me that I need not volunteer anymore. That was a disappointment to me.

In the last six years I have headed up a foundation my husband and I established called Y.E.S.S., an organization helping the city health department to provide supplements (vitamins and protein products) for the very poor. Eight hundred families a month were getting better attention and free supplements through eight to nine well-baby clinics. When I saw cases needing hospitalization or the care of a specialist, I would refer patients to the government hospital where hospitalization and specialist care were free. But the medicines were not! So Y.E.S.S. would help defray the cost of medications. Bedside prayer in the name of Jesus was a regular practice of mine as well as the other ladies of the foundation, who were mostly Muslim background believers.

Interviewer: Edna, in looking back was there any particular crisis that was hard for you? Was there perhaps a time when you questioned your call? And how did you get past it?

Edna: Yes. I think my first real crisis about the call came when I had to send my two older children away to boarding school. The youngest was only six. That was very difficult for me. God gave me the Scripture, Isaiah 43.10, "You are my witnesses, declares the Lord, and my servant whom I have chosen." God helped me through that difficult time. The younger two remained in home-schooling until we moved to a remote setting. I am happy to say that today all four of our children are following God. Their lives are successful and happy. God has watched over them. God has blessed us with twelve wonderful grandchildren who will be our focus for some time to come.

Interviewer: Share with us something of your retirement plans.

Edna: After 36 years of foreign missionary service, my husband and I are now considered officially retired. I am looking at options for supplementing our retirement income by hiring out for home-care nursing. Since our retirement home is in a region with many geriatric needs, my nursing skills will be in demand. Charles plans to do some missions consulting work. We will still be active.

Interviewer: Looking back over the years what are your dominant feelings about your years of ministry?

Edna: We gladly gave of our youth and service to the Master. We spent our lives doing what we delighted to do, answering the call of God. We have seen God in many wonderful ways. How precious few those 36 years now seem to be. We do rejoice in successful service to God, but our greater joy is in knowing Him and in our relationship with Him.

Interviewer: Will you ever quit being a missionary?

Edna: No! Never! The call of God brings with it a passion for souls that springs from Him alone and that call will be forever with us and can never be cancelled.

Editor's note:

It pleases us to honor Edna for her long and active career as a cross-cultural nurse, educator, wife, and mother of four. She is indeed a remarkable woman who just won't quit! We join with Charles in paying tribute to Edna for all the good works she has done and continues to do in the name of the Lord, and for the way she has quietly served Him all these years.

"Thy Father which seeth in secret shall reward thee openly." (Matt.6:6 KJV)